OCT   2008

Advance Praise for
How to Be a Sales Superstar

"This book elevates the profession of sales to its rightfully esteemed level. It was inspiring and motivational and I highly recommend it. It should be required reading for anyone already in sales or considering it as a career."

—Jim Connelly, author and keynote speaker,
the Napoleon Hill Institute

"The best way to sum up the information in this book is 'It just works!' I was very skeptical at first. The whole process put me way out of my comfort zone. We gave Mark Tewart's sales and management techniques a try and wow! what a difference it has made. Our gross profits went up between 30 and 50 percent depending on the department. The best part is of that is that our sales also increased over 25 percent and continue to increase. This has been the best process we have ever implemented and I have tried many. I would recommend this book, Mark Tewart, and Tewart Enterprises to everyone, except my competition. Bottom line, it just makes lots of money."

—Gary Minneman, General Manager, Sunshine
Toyota Battle Creek, Michigan

"Brilliantly written, completely engaging and one of THE most valuable books you will ever read (regardless of whether you are a salesperson or not). Mark delivers the essential guide for anyone who strives to be a superstar in their profession."

—Peggy McColl, *New York Times* bestselling author,
Your Destiny Switch

HOW TO BE A
Sales
Superstar

HOW TO BE A
Sales
Superstar

Break All the Rules and Succeed While Doing It

MARK TEWART

WILEY

John Wiley & Sons, Inc.

Published by John Wiley & Sons, Inc., Hoboken, New Jersey
Published simultaneously in Canada

For general information on our other products and services or for technical support, please contact our Customer Care Department within the United States at (800) 762-2974, outside the United States at (317) 572-3993 or fax (317) 572-4002.

Wiley also publishes its books in a variety of electronic formats. Some content that appears in print may not be available in electronic books. For more information about Wiley products, visit our web site at www.wiley.com.

Library of Congress Cataloging-in-Publication Data:

Tewart, Mark, 1961–
    How to be a sales superstar : break all the rules and succeed while doing it / Mark Tewart.
        p.   cm.
    Includes bibliographical references and index.
    ISBN 978-0-470-30096-1 (cloth)
        1. Selling.   I. Title.
    HF5438.25.T49   2009
    658.85—dc22
                                                                        2008020132

Printed in the United States of America

10   9   8   7   6   5   4   3   2   1

Contents

Foreword   *ix*

Acknowledgments   *xi*

Chapter 1   Sales is Not a Dirty Word   1

Chapter 2   Creating the Mind of a Sales Superstar   17

Chapter 3   Getting Your MBA—Massive Bank Account   35

Chapter 4   Getting What You Want Right Now!   55

Chapter 5   Put Time on Your Side   69

Chapter 6   It's All About the Attitude   83

Chapter 7   Lead Generation = $ Creation   97

Chapter 8   Dance With the One Who *Bought* You   119

Chapter 9   The Yellow Brick Road and Its Potholes   135

Chapter 10 Setting the Stage   153

Chapter 11 The Johnny Carson Principle   171

Contents

Chapter 12   I'll Take Door Number Two—Selection Time   183

Chapter 13   How to Get the Sale, Contract, and $ 197

About the Author   227

Index   229

Foreword

Selling is an art form of the most elaborate kind and it requires professional drive, passionate persistence, and positive dedication to craft the skill. I truly believe in my heart that success does not come to you, you must go to it. The path is well-traveled, but we must take the appropriate steps that will take us where we need—and want—to be. Today's entrepreneur and salesperson must capture the drive to succeed and work hard to rise to the top of their profession.

Mark Tewart has compiled a treasure-filled road map to what it takes to become the ultimate salesperson. Study it and benefit from the expertise and experience he outlines. Apply relevant concepts to your life, and prepare your mind for what lies ahead. Remember your sales career truly depends on the energy and education you invest in yourself. This book is an invaluable tool that will help you toward your goals.

Congratulations on giving your career an instant boost.

Nido Qubein
President, High Point University
Chairman, Great Harvest Bread Co.

Acknowledgments

This book was written for all the salespeople who go out everyday and make things happen. My hope is that this book will propel many to become sales superstars. I know what it's like to put blood, sweat, and tears into a sales profession. Those tears can often be from pain as well as joy. My wish for you is that you have a lot more tears of joy than pain. I respect, honor, and give a salute to all salespeople who give their ethical best everyday.

I want to thank the team at Wiley for bringing this book to life. I especially want to thank Matt Holt for believing that this would be a significant project and not just another book on sales. Thanks to Christine Moore for her countless hours of editing and making me look good. Also, thanks to Christine Kim and the whole marketing department and anyone else I might have missed.

Thanks to my assistant, Jaclyn Moreland for finding all my mistakes and putting up with me, my businesses, and all my wild ideas and projects.

Thanks to Ellen Neuborne who acted as my coach, editor, and friend during this project. Ellen spent countless hours reading, reviewing, and coaching me and my writing.

Thanks to all the mentors and people I have learned from, too numerous to mention here. If I were to mention them all individually, it would fill up this whole book. I have never believed that anyone is truly a self-made person. We are all a collection of ideas, teachings, and experiences involving others.

A special thanks to my family for their love and support. Without my family, this book or nothing else I have ever accomplished could have happened. Thanks to my wife Kim, my daughter Erin, and son Jake. Thanks to my parents, Raymond (Jake) Tewart and Mildred (Millie) Tewart. I was lucky to have parents that always believed in and supported me. God blessed me with great parents. Mom and Dad, I miss you daily.

A special thanks to my brother Gary Tewart. A great brother and mentor, you taught me great lessons in both your life and your death. Gary, I miss you greatly.

Thanks,
Mark R. Tewart

HOW TO BE A
Sales
Superstar

Sales is Not a Dirty Word

"Daddy, I Want to be a Salesperson"

The odds are pretty good that you never said this as a kid. Most kids want to grow up to be policemen, firemen, professional athletes, singers, actors, lawyers, and doctors. Not too many kids grow up dreaming of being a superstar salesperson. I have never witnessed children playing car dealership. When you were a child, what did you want to be when you grew up? How did that turn out for you? Many college graduates don't even wind up in the field that their degree is in. The good news is that the profession of sales can wind up being a lot better than your childhood dreams.

Most people back into sales as a career rather than choose it. Although that's not ideal, it's certainly okay, as that's the way that I and many others became salespeople. I call people like myself who have found themselves in sales careers *reluctant salespeople*. When you started your job, you probably weren't calling all of your friends and jumping up and down shouting that you had just gotten a position in sales.

1

Even though you picked up this book and maybe even bought it, there is a good possibility that you may not be that excited about sales at this moment. Not very many people are. Every year, polls and studies list sales as one of the least desired career paths. Very few colleges or technical schools have courses for selling. Most businesses don't offer formalized ongoing education for their salespeople.

The common frame of mind that salespeople share is that they are supposed to be naturally talented or self taught. Salespeople are continually hired and fired based upon the results they produce, and little to no effort is made to improve them. The motto, "Hire in masses and fire their asses" is still the prevalent, though ignorant mentality today. Salespeople are hired everyday without any type of screening, testing, or cogent analysis of their capabilities or talent for sales.

Here is the reality: Selling can, and *should,* be one of the noblest professions you can choose. Yes, that's right; I used the word noble. Among the definitions of noble in Wikipedia is the following: "Having honorable qualities; having moral eminence and freedom from anything petty, mean or dubious in conduct and character." Shouldn't that be part of the definition of salesperson? Shouldn't that be the norm, rather than the exception? Why wouldn't anyone aspire to be that person, and to have that description as part of their career? For all the titles I have—author, speaker, trainer, consultant, and entrepreneur—I am first and foremost a salesperson, and I always will be. I am proud of this title, and you should be as well.

Nothing Happens Unless Someone Sells Something

The world as you know it exists because of sales. If someone, somewhere, somehow is not selling every single day, you wouldn't have food to eat, a car to drive, or a house to live in. We can live a day without the skills of a lawyer, or even a doctor but you can't live even one single day without the skills of a salesperson.

Selling is one of the most important functions in our society. Capitalism and the advancement of any society are dependent upon sales. Everyone is a salesperson, and everyone sells everyday. In case you don't believe me, consider the following: If you are a parent, you sell "finishing dinner" to kids through the reward of dessert. If you are in a relationship, you sell your girlfriend on watching football in return for a nice dinner out. If you are in a career or have a job, you sell your boss on the effectiveness and productivity of what you do. If you don't have a job, you sell the person you interview with for a job that you are the best choice out of all the other applicants. Everyone is selling something everyday.

As a matter of fact, if you want to see fantastic sales skills in action, just watch kids. They are the best salespeople on earth. Kids understand the importance of selling the moment they arrive on the scene. They sell their tails off, and keep selling. If you watch kids, you'll notice that they ask directly for what they desire. They have not yet been programmed to think that this is somehow wrong or selfish. Kids rarely take no as a final answer, and they think about how to construct alternative persuasive arguments when their initial requests are refused. They try to create leverage in their urging through win-win questions and arguments. They believe strongly in what they want and believe that they deserve it. Usually it's parents, teachers, and other adults who try very hard to express to children that they shouldn't be selling. You were probably reprimanded, scolded, and scoffed at for most of your early selling efforts. Eventually you got the message loud and clear that selling was bad and something to be ashamed of. Managers and owners of businesses wonder why most people stink at selling; it's because they have been conditioned *not* to sell.

The first step in the journey to becoming a sales superstar will be to eliminate this conditioning. Whether you are someone who is considering sales for a career, a struggling salesperson, a salesperson looking to reach another level of success, or a sales superstar who wants to see if I am "spilling the beans" to your secrets, reading this book and utilizing what you learn will change your life.

I bet you have heard everyone of these phrases many times over: "I hate salespeople." "Salespeople are greedy." "Salespeople are pushy." "Salespeople just want your money." "Salespeople are all liars." "Salespeople are just uneducated pond scum that could not get jobs doing anything else." In the same vein, consider the following movies and plays that you may have seen or read: "Death of a Salesman," "Boiler Room," "Tin Men," "Cadillac Man," "Wall Street," "Glengarry Glenn Ross," and "Other People's Money." What images and emotions do you conjure up about salespeople and selling in general? They're not very positive, are they?

I would like for you to try to name one play, movie, TV show, or book where a salesperson is portrayed as a good person, or someone to be admired. I bet you can't do it. The first part of becoming a superstar salesperson is to understand the negative conditioning you and the rest of the world have been subjected to about sales. When too much garbage bombards your mind, your mind becomes garbage. You must drain your brain of the negative information that you have been sold and the lies that you have been told in regards to selling. And isn't there a bit of irony in the fact that you and the rest of the world may have a bad image of selling because of what you have been *sold,* and more importantly—what you have *bought?*

Many sales careers are stalled or derailed because salespeople never identify and get rid of the negative clutter in their brain about sales. If you are trying to be a successful salesperson, but your imagery, emotions, and teachings are in conflict with your mission; you will either fail or become a mediocre, frustrated, and unhappy salesperson. In other words, you will have joined the ranks of 90 percent of salespeople. I have seen a myriad of business cards with creative titles that try to eliminate identifying the person they represent as a salesperson—marketing director, customer representative, customer relations counselor, and new accounts manager. If you can't admit to being a salesperson or be proud to be a salesperson, you can't be a successful one. If you are a salesperson, try putting the title "Proud to Be a Salesperson" on your business cards. Let people know you are pleased with your title, and not ashamed. You will stand out in the crowd by doing so. Similarly, I have had numerous salespeople—through telemarketing or face-to-face selling—start off by telling me that they are not trying to sell me something. That's a part of their pitch. They are liars, however, because they are, and *should,* be trying to sell me something. Let me give you a tip: It's okay to sell something, and it's okay to declare it.

I can count on my fingers and toes the so-called sales gurus and trainers who wanted my company to sell their sales seminars because they didn't feel comfortable selling themselves, and they would rather have someone else do the selling. The truth is that they didn't believe they could do what they were teaching. You must embrace selling as something you should do, want to do, and can do and not run from it. You must be able to embrace whatever it is that you are selling. A business professor from Carnegie Mellon once told me that the sales course he taught through an entrepreneur program was the one course he was sure every attendee would eventually use. Therefore, he thought it was the most important. Ask any successful business owner the key to their success, and if they don't tell you that it's the ability to sell, then they just haven't realized it yet.

In his best-selling book, *Rich Dad Poor Dad* (TechPress, 1997), author Robert Kiyosaki recounts how after his college graduation, his so-called "Rich Dad" and mentor had counseled him to take a job in sales with a company that offered a good sales training program. His advice was that sales would be the most important tool that Mr. Kiyosaki would use being an entrepreneur. Meanwhile, Mr. Kiyosaki's own father—the so-called "Poor Dad" who was a college professor and administrator—was shocked at the idea, and thought that this was beneath his son. The Rich Dad had a less formal education than the Poor Dad, but he had experienced far superior results in the business and financial world. Much like myself and many other salespeople, Mr. Kiyosaki backed into sales. His initial thoughts and feelings were that sales might be beneath him or a waste of his college education.

I have witnessed situations like Mr. Kioyski's time and time again. Years ago, as a general manager at an automobile dealership, I had a salesperson with tons of talent and potential quit his sales job with our company. The reason he quit his sales job was to take an entry level position with a rental car company. He informed me that he wanted to use his college education. Although I am sure that the company he went to work for is a fine company that provided him with many opportunities, I was positive that this young salesperson was simply embarrassed to be a salesperson, and believed that it was beneath him. The prospect of being a rental clerk was more exciting to him than being a salesperson. The truth is that he probably learned more about the business world and used more of his education in six months of selling cars than he might ever use in the rental car business.

I see more people in sales than in any other profession who are only in selling "until something else comes along." Sometimes I believe there are more admitted career cab drivers in New York and Los Angeles than there are admitted career salespeople. If you get into a sales career "to check it out, you will check out." In other words, you will fail due to a lack of commitment. If you want to do more than "check it out," somewhere, somehow, you must truly commit to sales as a career. You must understand that selling is not a low-level profession. Being a salesperson puts you at the top of the heap, not the bottom.

"Sales" is Not a Dirty Word!

You must be proud of what you do. You must morally, ethically, mentally, and emotionally "buy into" sales as a fantastic career. Selling is not something you can do half-assed or with unenthused commitment. The good news is that there are very few professions that can provide you with as much fun, freedom, excitement, adrenaline, competition, income, and wealth potential as sales. I have spent a lot of time and ink in the beginning of this book discussing the mindset of acceptance and exuberance for selling. The reason for this is because without your total mental and emotional commitment, everything else I share in this book will only lead to mediocrity or failure.

This book is not about how to be good at sales. This book is not about how to be better at sales. This book is about how to be a Sales Superstar. This book is about how to make huge incomes from your sales efforts and get rich. If you don't believe in this premise, do not read the rest of the book. There are tons of sales books that will gain you mediocrity; I only want superstars. Life is too short to aim low and live a daily uninspired existence that is average and frustrating.

Secrets Sales Superstars Don't Want You to Know

Selling is both the highest and lowest paying profession on earth. Unfortunately, the majority of salespeople are in the low end. The good news is that if you do the exact opposite of what 95 percent of salespeople do you will succeed and can become wealthy in doing so. Let's look at what it means, by definition, to be different in your approach or viewpoint.

Contrary: Opposed, opposite in nature, altogether different.
Contrarian: A person who takes an opposing view, especially one who rejects the majority opinion as in economic matters.

Several Native American tribes such as the Cheyenne, Crow, and Iroquois had warrior sects called Contraries or Contrary Warriors. The Contrary Warriors were different from their peers in their nature, often acting in direct opposition to the conventional tribe wisdom. Despite their controversial actions, they were thought to be very wise warriors, and were said to act like lightning in a storm. The Contraries became one with the sacred power they most feared. They liberated themselves from conventional and hallowed fears. As you look through history, you will likely make the same observation of most successful people. Successful people, like the Contrary Warriors, think for themselves and don't blindly follow the teachings and thoughts of the masses.

I have been in sales for most of my life and have spent a lot of time, money, and effort to study superstar salespeople and entrepreneurs. Because of what I have studied, learned, and taken action on, I have had a lot of success and made quite a bit of money in sales. I have often found that superstar salespeople take a Contrarian approach to sales and their business. Following the masses seldom leads to success in sales, just like following the masses seldom leads to success in any endeavor. When everyone else in the marketplace buys stocks, real estate, or anything else in false exuberance, the Contrarian investor patiently waits to pounce on the opportunities created when the market turns and winds up picking the bones of the dead carcasses from the ignorant masses. When the world was busy buying tech stocks and looking to get rich quick, the "Oracle of Omaha" Warren Buffett refused to follow the trend and buy businesses he did not understand. No matter how much the so-called experts blasted him as being a "has-been" or out of touch, he took the Contrarian Approach. Mr. Buffett stayed invested with companies such as Coca Cola and Dairy Queen, instead of the sexier tech stocks that most people thought would bring quick riches. Warren Buffet never followed the masses, and through an approach that seemed contrarian to many investors at the time, wound up with substantial profits while the tech stocks sank.

The entrepreneur who follows the masses and opens up the tenth coffee shop in a small town because it seems cool and is what everybody is doing; winds up failing and losing money. Unsuccessful salespeople are like lemmings. Lemmings are the animals that blindly follow one another in a line right off a cliff to their death. On the other hand, the Contrarian entrepreneur looks for the niche opportunity created because of all the new coffee shops, and succeeds because he goes where no one else is going.

Thirty years ago when I began my career, I made note of who was the very best in sales—who the "superstars" were. I observed that they made much more money than the rest of the salespeople, and I noticed that they broke all the so-called rules of selling. The superstars didn't think or act the same way as the rest of the salespeople. The sales superstars did not wait for customers or even expect the business they worked for to provide them with leads. The sales superstars knew that the REAL money is in their customer base, and did not ignore this. Sales superstars didn't use the same sales presentations or customer qualifying techniques that everyone else uses. The sales superstars understood their customers, and they used this understanding to bend the rules in the selling system or in the companies they worked for.

Often, sales superstars' managers can't stand them. The superstars are often thought of as uncontrollable, and they don't tow the company line. The superstars are often called "mavericks" or "high maintenance." Those same managers tell new salespeople not to emulate superstars because "they are different, and everyone can't do what they do." The truth is those managers are looking for people they can control. Superstar salespeople tend to threaten weak managers. They are often condemned because they do things differently. But of course doing things differently is what makes them superstars.

When you become a selling superstar, be prepared to deal with the jealously that you will incur from managers and fellow salespeople. Just remember that no one can keep you from being successful except you. You are in charge of your destiny. Be happy that you have critics, it means you have success to be envied. Critics don't pick on the weak; they don't have anything to gain in doing so. In Australia, this is called the "Tall Poppy Syndrome." When one poppy grows taller than the other poppies, the others begin to squeeze and smother the tall poppy to keep it from growing taller than the rest. This way, all the poppies stay the same height. That's exactly what will happen to you if you let it. Don't be a poppy. Allow yourself to grow despite the squeezing and smothering you may experience.

I am not telling you to be a troublemaker, or to break rules for the sake of breaking rules. I am not telling you to purposely be a thorn in your manager's side. However, I am telling you that to be successful in anything, you have to make tough decisions and follow a path that may not always be popular, and will most certainly often be Contrarian.

During my time as general manager of the automobile dealership, I held a meeting one day and asked my sales team, "What if we started doing everything differently? What if we did the exact opposite of everything we currently do? What if our meeting and greeting of our customers was opposite of what it is now? What if our customer qualifying process was opposite? What if our presentation process was opposite? What if our negotiation process was opposite? What if our marketing was opposite?"

Several of the salespeople asked me why I was asking this. I told them that I felt that the industry was stale. I believed that we had been selling cars the same way for over fifty years. I told them that I thought our customers were becoming more educated and were changing, and that we and the rest of the business would have to change with them. I said that customers would simply not put up with the nonsense that they had experienced in the past when they shopped for and bought vehicles. I told our sales team that we could either be leading this charge, or we could fall behind. I said that although we were currently number one in sales in our marketplace, that stagnation would eventually lead to trouble for us.

This book, and a lot of what's in it, comes directly or indirectly from that one question I asked my sales team many years ago: "What if we started doing everything differently?" I began to observe every step of the sales process from the simple meet and greet down to negotiations. I began to use trial and error in seeing if my Contrarian approach would work. Some things worked really well, while others had to be tweaked.

The bottom line is that one simple question led to major changes, which led to big success. Since that time I have applied that same thought process in helping salespeople from all kinds of businesses representing all kind of industries.

The same principle applies to your sales success. Here is the truth—much of what you've learned is wrong. Most of what sales trainers are pushing is useless. You may have sat for hours in training sessions writing down everything that you hear because you're hoping that one of these gurus has the "magic button." You are looking for the one line that's going to miraculously overcome objections and help close every sale as easy as one, two, three. The truth is that most of those gurus are peddling old-fashioned information. They're only teaching twenty-five tips, or ten rules, or a "road map" to sales success. That's the old school approach. The reality today is that sales success takes more than sales skills. You need proficiency beyond the "Tie-Down Method," or "Qualifying Your Customer." You need more than just a networking group meeting and thank-you cards. You must have access to what's working in today's market, and you need to use what works in this century. You need the mindset and real world knowledge that are going to make you a superstar. Selling is a job that demands a new and improved tool kit. I'm not talking about tricks or slippery systems to get a customer to cave in. These tools are ones that influence you not the customer. These are the tools that make you better. And when you get better, it's amazing how much better your customers get.

That's what this book is about. It's about throwing out all the old-school rules of sales, or at least being willing to question them. It's the Contrarian Guide to being a sales superstar. In all fairness, I must give you a disclaimer that not all sales education, techniques, or training are bad; some are quite good, and still usable today. However, many are not. The idea is that everything is up for review. Nothing is sacred just because it's the way you were taught or the way you have always done it.

This book will teach you what to do, when to do it, how to do it, and most importantly, why to do it. Everything you learn in this book may be explained in a manner that is probably opposite of what you have been taught. As a matter of fact, what I tell you to do may sometimes be the wrong thing to do; but doing the wrong thing is part of success.

Continually testing, tinkering, and improving are all parts of the equation that brings about sales success. To be a sales superstar, you have to be willing to make mistakes more often and fail more often. Your failures are a big part of your sales education. Learn to embrace the bumps in the road, but don't accept them as permanent.

The world of sales is a not a perfect one, and nobody in it has absolute answers. Selling is part science and part art, and it can never be fully mastered. That is exactly why selling is such a fun, exciting, and fulfilling profession. Very few people reach sales superstar status; that is also why it pays so well. Am I trying to scare you by telling you this? If this scares you, then pick another profession. Selling is not for the faint of heart.

The Millionaire Maker—What do you need to be a Sales Superstar?

- **Sales Skills:** You don't need a magic button to overcome objections. You need to understand why people have objections in the first place, and how to eliminate eight out of ten objections before they ever occur. Sales today is about being proactive, not reactive. You must be able to recognize an objection even when your customer is not verbalizing one. Sales skills include abilities such as how to present and demonstrate your product or service, how to take or make sales calls, or how to negotiate professionally.

When most people think of a salesperson, they picture a slick, fast talking individual with all of the answers who manipulates someone into buying something, whether they want it or not. Although sales superstars are excellent persuaders, they are equally as good at helping people find the solutions to their problems. The best superstar salespeople I have ever seen were great not just because of their sales skills, but because of the other skills listed below. Instead of learning fifty ways to close a sale, why not try writing down the four most frequent objections you get, and why they come up. With a little thought and preparation, you just might be able to head off many of the objections. Think like a Contrarian. Reverse the mindset.

Here's a Shocker. . .

Improving your sales skills will help you tremendously, but this alone will not make you a sales superstar. That's what most salespeople and sales training focus on; but it totally misses the mark. You must become great at the following skills to become a sales superstar; the ability to master these skills is the mark of a true Millionaire Maker.

- **People Skills:** Whenever I interview potential salespeople and they say, "I love people," it frankly makes me want to puke. Yes, you must want to help your customers solve their problems, you must TLC—Think Like a Customer, and you must really care for your customers. However, sales superstars rarely become superstars because of their love of humanity. Mother Theresa was a great salesperson for humanity, but she probably would not have done well selling computers.

Although salespeople do not have to be great humanitarians, they must practice good human relations skills, such as listening. When your customer speaks, you must know what they are saying, what they are trying to say, and what they really mean. Old-school techniques rely solely on what to say back, which only makes your customers mad. Sales superstars have excellent listening skills. They observe people, are highly intuitive, and have the capacity to read and truly understand people.

- **Life Skills:** These are the everyday skills that separate you from the masses. You must be precise with what you think, what you do, when you do it, and why you are doing it. You must understand abundance versus scarcity. The world is an abundant universe with unlimited resources. Money is not limited, sales are not limited, and customers are not limited. Proper life skills will allow you to tap into this abundance at any time.

How to gain and maintain a sales superstar attitude is part of honing these life skills. Figuring out what to do with your day that leads to the most bang for your buck is a life skill. Knowing how to trigger strong sales persistence when your competition has already quit is a life skill. These skills are not rah-rah sales tips or how to do your to-do list. These are real, live, actionable ideas. For example, in the Action Management section of this book, you will learn that what you have been taught by time management gurus can make you a slave and keep you broke. In the Goal Setting section, you will learn why 95 percent of salespeople fail or don't reach their potential because of life skills alone.

Superstar salespeople figure out early on that you must work as hard, or even harder, on yourself as you do on your business. Successful people are eager learners. They understand that you never stop learning, and that you are never too successful to learn. Education must become a regular part of your day. If you are a sales manager and you interview sales recruits, ask them how they feel about continuing education. Ask them what they have done to educate themselves lately. If you are faced with a person who can't demonstrate a desire for learning, then don't hire them. These people turn out to be prima donna low producers.

- **Marketing Skills:** Lots of people tell you how to market yourself. Every day I read more about the power of marketing, or branding, or some other new idea that keeps salespeople broke. Showing up at cocktail parties or business networking breakfasts and handing out your business card is no way to market yourself. Chances are, the salesperson at these events has too much time on their hands, and the sales superstars are not there, because they are out making sales. If the sales superstars are at these events, they have a better game plan than handing out boring business cards that fail to market them and that lack incentives for someone to take action.

This book will show you low- to no-cost marketing techniques to make you money. To thrive in sales, you must become a student and practitioner of emotional direct response marketing. You have to have a constant flow of leads that you create. For over one hundred years, traditional sales training has tried to teach you what to do to become great with customers. However, you first have to be great at *getting* customers, so that you have customers to be great *with*. Without customers, you fail. You have to acquire customers, and just as importantly—you have to keep them. Most salespeople worry so much about getting new customers that they forget to do what is necessary to keep the ones they already have.

I will cover all of these skills in detail in the following chapters. Why listen to me? Because I've been there. I've lived it, and I still do. I have been a successful salesperson from a young age. I know what it's like to be broke and need to sell something just to eat and pay rent. I know the challenges you face. I have gone from being broke and homeless to being wealthy and successful because of sales. I am not a sales professor or some has-been sales hack that talks about success, but has never experienced it. I have sold many millions of dollars of products and services and have risen from the bottom to the top. So have countless others using my methods and ideas. I have created several successful businesses using the exact methodology that I will share in this book.

Salespeople are not born; they are made. I don't believe in the natural born salesperson. I have had people tell me that Michael Jordan was a natural born basketball player. Michael Jordan may have been born with immense talent and gifts, but he was cut from his high school basketball team. Even he had to practice and work his rear off to become great. Don't use excuses and allow thoughts of mediocrity to keep you from superstar status.

Sales superstars learn early on that they have to work as hard *on* the business as they do *in* the business. Every day, your thoughts and actions must be directed toward growing your business exponentially, and how to automate a large percentage of your everyday functions. You can learn to automate many parts of your marketing, customer follow-up, and other functions. You can learn to grow your business by expanding your efforts through others and outsourcing. The average salesperson will often complain that they don't have enough time. He does not believe that he can find alternate resources for anything he desires to do or have done. The average salesperson waits for things to happen and hopes and prays for success. I use the anagram "HOPE" to describe this person's actions, which can be defined as **H**aving **O**ptimistic **P**redictions and **E**motions. Although having hope is the first step, there is a saying, "Pray, but move your feet." Hope can only get you so far.

I have seen superstar salespeople who were not considered attractive—I definitely fall into that category. I have seen superstar salespeople that were not smooth talkers. I have seen superstar salespeople that had foreign dialects and were very hard to understand, who were not well-educated, and who were not necessarily nice people. There is not a cookie cutter formula for superstar salespeople. Superstars come in all shapes, sizes, and personalities.

So eliminate any excuses, get rid of any preconceived ideas, eradicate the mental baggage; and let's begin your journey to becoming a sales superstar.

2

Creating the Mind of a Sales Superstar

The Most Important Decision of My Life

On November 19, 2005—one day after having surgery to have my tonsils removed—I was diagnosed with squamous cell carcinoma cancer. I would compare the way I felt when I received the news to being numbed in the dentist's chair. But instead of just my mouth, this news had numbed my whole body. For twenty minutes, I experienced a barrage of all kinds of thoughts and emotions—shock, anger, asking "why me?", and sadness.

However, after twenty minutes of running the gamut of helpless emotions, I made a big decision. I decided to live. I realized my initial reaction was not supporting me. I resolved right then and there to switch all beliefs and actions to those of support, complete cure, and total health and wellness. And the moment that I made that decision, I was cured.

On January 31, 2006, I received my 33rd and final daily radiation treatment. I am now cancer free. I did not need the doctor to declare that

17

for me. I had already made that decision from the day of diagnosis. I had even told my doctor that at my first appointment.

For my whole life, I have believed in the power of the mind. Our ability to shape our own life's experiences from our thoughts and emotions is undeniable. Nothing is as powerful as your personal philosophy in life, and you get to decide what your personal philosophy is.

In my lifetime, I have been both poor and rich. I have had both sad and happy times. I have lived through tragedies and triumphs. One thing that has never wavered has been my mental approach to whatever has come towards me. Nothing can generate wealth and abundance in any segment of your life, including your sales, more than your attitudes and thoughts. I have seen financially rich people with great poverty of mind, and I have seen people with monetary struggles who exhibit an attitude of abundance. Wealth and possessions can be lost in an instant, but nothing, and nobody, can take away your mind and your choice of thought.

Whenever friends or relatives would begin to discuss my disease, they would focus on how very unfair they felt that it was, especially since I am a lifetime non-smoker. Ninety-nine percent of the particular cancer that I had occurs in heavy smokers. Because of these facts, I also initially dwelled on how unjust I felt my illness was. However, I had to make a decision not to focus on whether it was fair or not; instead I concentrated on what could be done to move forward and get healthy.

I decided to research my disease. I wanted to be empowered in my decisions, and I knew that knowledge would create this power. I created a regimented approach that included traditional treatment along with a focus on beneficial nutrition, supplements, whole body detoxification, exercise, proper rest, mental imaging, and prayer. Some of these approaches were never mentioned by conventional medicine practitioners. However, I made the decision to be in charge of my knowledge and my actions, and to take the steps that I felt were necessary to beat the disease.

After witnessing many people receive treatment for cancer, and losing both of my parents to this disease as well, I am more convinced than ever that attitude and power of mind makes a difference in everything you do in life. I am also convinced that the way in which I approached the disease made the difference in my personal outcome. In sales, the most important sale that is made is in first making sure that *you* are sold on what you believe and what you are doing. The decision of what attitude to take, and which philosophy to follow, is the most important choice of your life.

Identifying Your Roadblocks

I have often sat with salespeople that had, up to that point, experienced mediocre results in their careers. I would ask them what their goals were, and they usually responded with a large number or monetary goal. Most of the time, the expression on their faces told me that they didn't really believe in their goal, and that they were just trying to please me, rather than themselves.

And while I would never shoot down anyone's goal, I want people to have goals that they make for *themselves.* I want salespeople to have big goals and big dreams, and more importantly I want you to reach them, and to believe that you *can* reach them. When I would ask salespeople what they were going to do differently in the future that would lead to a large increase in sales and money, they would reply with a few common answers. "I am going to work harder," "I am going to work more hours," "I am going to have a better attitude," and "I am going to follow up more thoroughly with my customers." Even though all of these answers are very good, I find that the enthusiasm for those actions runs out quickly. I also find that physical stamina wanes just as quickly. I think it was Vince Lombardi who said that "Fatigue makes cowards of us all." Why can't you just do those things that you declare? The reason is roadblocks.

A positive philosophy is a requirement to be successful in sales and in life. To have a successful philosophy, you must first identify your mental roadblocks. In other words, it's okay to declare that you are going to be successful. This may actually be the first step. But you have to identify what has kept you from being successful already. Words are only cheap if you let them be; they must have some meaning behind them in order to carry value. It's fine to admit that you have roadblocks; everybody has them, and recognizing them is the first step towards eliminating them.

Let's Determine Your Roadblocks

I want you to list, on a piece of paper, the setbacks that you have experienced in your life. Include any bad or negative things that have happened, like the time you didn't reach a goal you had set, or a time you were embarrassed when you tried to do something. Think all the way back to your childhood and write down anything you can recall, no matter how small or insignificant it may seem. Don't edit or judge; just write.

After you have listed as many setbacks as you can recall in numerical order, I want you examine these setbacks, and try to come up with a list of possible reasons for each of them. See if you can discern any patterns. Your life tends to follow a series of patterns. To change your future, you have to change these patterns. This is definitely not easy; since patterns are habitual you create and put them on autopilot. If your autopilot is continually driving you into the ground or sending you to undesired locations, then why do you still allow it to lead you? The answer is that your autopilot pattern has become comfortable to you.

Look at the following list. It is a compilation of elements that might affect the outcome of any given situation. Now, go back and look at your own list of setbacks, and determine which elements on the list might have instigated them. For example, let's say that the setback you experienced was that you did not get an account that you desired. Looking down this list, you may stop at the very first item, which is education. You may decide that a lack of education or training kept you from getting the account. So put that setback in the education category. Continue to go through all of your setbacks and identify which element on the list you consider responsible for the negative outcome. Then, look at your paper and see if there is a pattern? Do you have one reason that comes up time and time again as an element in your setbacks?

1. Education or training
2. Reward
3. Punishment
4. Natural ability
5. Intelligence

 6. Background
 7. Desperation
 8. Coaching or a mentor
 9. Parental guidance
10. Likes
11. Dislikes
12. Practice
13. Enthusiasm
14. Circle of influence
15. Persistence
16. Personality
17. Time

Now I want to get a little Freudian with you. I want you to think back, beginning with your childhood, and ask yourself if the dominant and recurring reason for your setbacks is because of something you have seen, heard, or experienced that greatly influenced you. I am sure that some of you are reading this and are saying, "Oh man, give me a break. What a bunch of psychobabble." However, I invite you to open up your mind and be patient. What have you got to lose? Chances are you are either new to selling, or that you aren't getting the results you want anyway. This exercise can't hurt you, but it might just get you to think.

The majority of us are pattern-repeaters. We tend to do things over and over. This is partly because of what is known as the Law of Familiarity, which comes from Gestalt psychology. Simply put, this law states that people tend to see or group things together based upon familiarity. Their behavior tends to follow those same patterns, and when this happens, they enter the autopilot stage.

Examining your thoughts, beliefs, actions, and their results can be a scary proposition. It is admittedly easier just to watch TV, hang out with your buddies doing football pools, or go to Starbucks (or engage in what-ever other mind numbing autopilot habits we form). Go to any Starbucks in the world, and I will show you at least one unsuccessful salesperson hanging out. These wannabe or afraid-to-be salespeople have formed a habit of going to Starbucks first thing in their work day. It's like a barrier that they have set up to keep from taking important actions. When they get there, they decide to do their paperwork. Then they have to check email, instant messages, text messages, MySpace, read the paper, and make a call to their spouse. Pretty soon, its noon and they really haven't hit a lick; but they are going to lunch. Why do these people spend so much time essentially doing nothing? Because of fear. They feel unidentified fear, and their time-wasting, unnecessary activities allow them to form roadblocks to facing their fear.

If you examine all of the potential reasons I listed for setbacks, you'll notice that they are all just a front for fears and negative emotions. Somewhere, somehow, you too have likely picked up such fears. Negative emotions like these can maneuver you like a racecar driver. Although you are in the car, you are no longer steering; you are simply along for the ride. Unfortunately, this driver always sends you smack into the wall.

It's only when you identify your setbacks and patterns, and their reasons and emotional roots that you can begin to correct them. You can't fix them by working harder, smarter, or longer, or by doing anything else that you brainwash yourself into believing will help. And you certainly cannot fix them by avoiding them and focusing your energy instead on mindless tasks. Doing all of these things is like trying to fix a bumper falling off a car by putting a Band-Aid on it.

I am going to have you make another list; only this time I want you to list your biggest and most persistent fears. Be honest with yourself; avoiding the truth won't help. Ask yourself the following questions: "If these fears came true, what is the worst that would happen? What would I stand to lose?" Then ask yourself if you would survive this. You will find that you have chronic fears that have grown into monsters, and that you most likely *would* survive the worst that would happen.

Everyone has, at one time or another, worried about a potential negative fate to the point that it becomes extremely detrimental. Such constant worry causes them to create and attract the very thing that they don't want. If you worry about not making a sale or not hitting your quota, that is exactly what will happen, because you are bringing these thoughts into your reality. All images and messages you send out from your brain, both good and bad, will be answered. Have *you* ever experienced a fear so all-encompassing that it became a reality as much as if it had actually come to pass? Ninety-eight percent of your fears never even come close to becoming reality. However, in your mind, they are becoming emotional and even physical realities. Take notice that your dominant fears seem to be the ones you concentrate on over and over. You have essentially become comfortable with those fears. They are like comfort food, because you turn to them for emotional security even though they aren't good for you . . . Now let's get rid of them forever.

Destroying Your Roadblocks

"It's not about the money, it's about the doggone money."

– David Burgin, Consultant with Tewart Management Group Inc.

Here's another exercise: Take a piece of paper and write down the earliest memories you have of or lessons you learned about money. (I bet some of you could write a list ten pages long.)

Do any of them resemble the teachings or sayings that I am sure many of you have often heard?

"Money isn't everything."
"Money does not buy happiness."
"Money doesn't grow on trees."
"You have to work HARD to get money."
"A penny saved is a penny earned."
"Money is the root of all evil."
"You have to have money to make money."
"The rich get richer and the poor get poorer."
"What do you think we are made of, money?"
"If you work that hard for money you can't spend time with your family."
"Don't be greedy."

"Rich people are snobs."
"Rich people stick together."
"The rich kid goes to college and the poor kid goes to work."

Let's examine a few items from your earliest memories of money, and consider the meaning of these sayings.

"Money Isn't Everything"

As professional speaker Zig Ziglar says, "Money isn't everything but it ranks right up there with oxygen." This saying is usually used as an excuse as to why the person saying it doesn't have money. Money doesn't have to be *everything,* but it does not have to interfere with everything you cherish. It can simply give you freedom of choice to pursue more of what you desire.

"Money Does Not Buy Happiness"

Neither does poverty. I have been broke, and I have had money; and I choose money. I've noticed that when people are worrying about paying bills or trying to get their next meal, they don't seem too happy. Happiness is a choice, but in most societies, money gives you more choices. When you say money does not buy you happiness, who are you kidding?

Considering the following story: There is an old fashioned, country-style restaurant just one mile from my home. I eat there quite often and I enjoy it. The food is really good, the prices are fair, and the service is very friendly and homespun. The restaurant has one particular waitress who I notice is always working her tail off. By her own admission, she is financially broke. The interesting thing is that a few years ago she won a couple of million dollars in the lottery, which she immediately proceeded to spend and gamble away. Her health and personal habits declined. She now says, "Oh well, money does not make you happy." She is right in what she says; money just tends to allow people to be more of who they already really are. Happiness is a choice. Once again, she is someone who is using this phrase as a common refrain to allow herself to be broke.

I believe she was uncomfortable with the picture she had of herself as a person with money. All of her life, she had a self and society-imposed image of herself that included poverty and struggle. Money did not change or better that image. Her self-image of struggle and poverty led her to get rid of the money, in order to get back to the state with which was she familiar and where she felt comfortable. The phrase "money does not buy happiness" was simply the outward excuse she used to allow this inner image of poverty and struggle to eliminate her short-term riches.

"Money Does Not Grow on Trees"

The government prints money every single day. There isn't any difference between a printing press or a tree except for a belief system and effort. Money is simply a tangible form of value: money received = value given. The more value you create in yourself and share with the world, the more money you will receive. When you accept that fact and take action on it, you will see a dramatic increase in your sales and cash flow. When you chase paper, you will push it away; so don't worship the paper. But do become dogged in the ideas, value, and service that create the paper currency. No matter where money comes from, it's what you do to make yourself valuable to others that attracts it. The phrase "money does not grow on trees" implies that money is not abundant and it's not easy to get. However, money is abundant, and money flows to value. The question is not if money is scarce, but if you are valuable enough to attract it.

"Money Is the Root of all Evil."

This may be one of the most misquoted parts of the Bible. Money *itself* is not the root of all evil; it's the love of money. Big difference. This inaccurate quote equates money and making money to greed. Attracting money by increasing your value is a positive form of value exchange, and has nothing to do with evil or sinister actions. The attraction of money is not limited to greed. Only the negative mindset of people trying to acquire money creates the evil. Believing that money is the root of all evil means that someone has to lose for you to gain and attracting money is not a win-lose proposition. I fully believe that you could take everything from me and parachute me into anywhere and I would attract money and success. A belief system that appreciates money is based upon abundance, value, and positive exchange.

Television and Movies Portrayal of Money

As another exercise, I want you to list some movies you have seen where the rich character was portrayed as bad, villainous, greedy, snobbish, or lacking good character. Below are just a few examples.

"Trading Places"
"The Toy"
"Wall Street"
"Indecent Proposal"
"The Talented Mr. Ripley"
"Other People's Money"
"Greedy"

Now, if I were to ask you to make a list of movies where the rich person is depicted as a hero, good person, or shown in a good light—how many could you list? Probably not many. For every one movie made with a positive plot line, there are hundreds, maybe thousands, made where a rich person was portrayed negatively.

Now, try the same exercise with TV shows.

"Dallas"
"The Real Housewives of Orange County"
"Fresh Prince of Bel Air"
"Dirty Sexy Money"

You get the picture. Rich person = bad person.

Let's say that you were raised in the United States, which is, for arguments sake, the richest country in the world. In this richest country, you likely grew up being bombarded by messages, images, and teachings telling you that it was bad to have money or be rich. On the other hand, immigrants tend to see opportunity to build and provide a better life for themselves and their families. Money is the form of exchange used to seize these opportunities. The same limiting or negative images and messages of money simply do not exist in the minds of most immigrants. It is interesting that many of the images and messages we receive come from the movie, TV, and entertainment field, which itself makes so much money and creates so much wealth. The entertainment industry as a whole tends to denigrate the very thing that feeds and grows their own industry.

In the United States, people are often comfortable being comfortable. This is precisely why an immigrant to the United States is nine times more likely statistically to become a millionaire than a person who was born in the United States. For the average person who was born in the United States, your perception is not the perceived reality of the average immigrant. For the immigrant, the United States is still the land of opportunity. Where the native born American complains about a lack of things; the immigrant often sees opportunity.

A Warning about Saving

Let me now address any saying or teaching about savings in relation to money. Saving and investing is very important. When you are a good steward of money it leads to better sales and wealth. However, you must remember that the world is abundant, and that there is never a lack of money. You can be a meager salesperson and through average wages, prudent saving, and smart investing, become wealthy. You will spend most of your life acquiring this wealth, and if this is what you want, then that's great. However, that is not what this book is about. This book is about becoming a sales superstar. This is about going to the top and getting there at warp speed. Gradually climbing to the top or saving your way through life are not methods you should be adopting. You are looking for, expecting, and creating impressive and immediate results. Money is to be used as a positive instrument, and not hoarded.

Try the following: First, refuse to ever again use the sayings or teachings of money that limit you and deter you from success. I'm sorry to tell you this but it's possible that your parents, although well-intentioned, may have harmed you more than helped you with those handed down limitations. Both of my parents have passed away, and I loved them dearly. They were great parents, and good people. But God love them, they were wrong as far as money goes. I spent a long time fighting the battle that started with the teachings they ingrained in me. Most likely you have to do this as well. It's time—just let them go.

Breaking Through . . .

You now know that to become a superstar salesperson, you must identify your roadblocks and then break through them. Many of you reading this book right now are thinking, "Just give me the Magic Pill. Teach me the perfect closes. Tell me exactly what to say." Later in this book, we cover all of those sales skills and so-called Magic Pills. However, those skills won't mean squat without the information that we are covering here. Without these first steps, you will work harder and harder to get the same or worse results with a lot more frustration. You will unintentionally push away more sales and money than you will ever make.

Let's take a look at a metaphor that I have used for years in trying to assist people in getting past their roadblocks. I call this the "Game of Your Life."

Imagine that you are in a football game. Every play is analogous to an event that occurs in your life. In this game, you are the star quarterback. You have teammates, and they are the people in your life—your spouse or significant other, your kids, siblings, bosses, co-workers, and anyone else that comes into your world. As the star quarterback of the game, you want to have a say in the plays that are called. You want control over how things go, and you want to influence the outcome of the game. But at the same time, your teammates feel the same way; they also want to have a say in how things go and how this game ends up. Sometimes what your teammates want and what you want, and how you each go about getting this are the same—and sometimes they aren't.

A team has to have a coach. In this scenario, the coach has the final say on the play calling. Imagine that your conscious brain is you as the star quarterback. Your teammates are the oft-competing messages going to the brain. The coach is actually your subconscious. The coach listens to the messages from you, the quarterback (and the conscious choice) and to the messages from your teammates. He collects all other messages and images, and makes the final decision.

Here is the bottom line and the message I want to get across here, you make conscious choices. You choose your goals and dreams and what you want to do. However, your subconscious may be receiving conflicting messages from everyone and everything else. When your conscious and subconscious don't align—or when the coach and the quarterback don't agree—and the competing messages are stronger than what your conscious wants, you will sabotage your own selling, goals, hopes, and dreams. You can work increasingly harder, and you will never get what you want. You are only going to become frustrated and begin to adopt a defeatist attitude. You will be adding evidence to your subconscious, which validates this failure as correct.

I have yet to meet a person where this scenario has not played out in at least one aspect of their life at one time or another. The good news is that it's okay to experience this, as long you recognize what is happening and understand the power of it. Then, you can begin to work on never letting yourself sabotage your own sales success again.

Creating the Mind of the Sales Superstar

Let's identify what you must do to move past your limitations. Have you ever read a letter with a P.S.—a postscript? I call it an "Oh, by the way" statement or question, something that has come to mind after the main points have been addressed. Whether or not you realize it, you have P.S.

statements attached to your goals. They are those nasty, conflicting images that your teammates are sending to your coach, or subconscious. One way to identify them is to write down a goal, and then just sit still and think, feel, and observe your body, feelings, and thoughts.

Are you seeing, in your mind's eye, little thought bubbles that say "I could do that, but . . ." or, "I would do that, except . . ." or, "I will do that *when*. . ."? These are examples of the P.S. statements your subconscious is feeding your brain, thereby telling it that it's okay to go ahead and fail, or not to try at all. To create a superstar mind, you must train your brain. You must give your brain overwhelming evidence of a potential positive result. Here are some ways to do this when you are writing down your goals:

- Pay attention to those P.S. thoughts and feelings and write them down.
- Rewrite those P.S. statements as the opposite of what they currently are—i.e., "I *will* do this, and . . ."
- Eradicate the negative and write the positive, eliminating the fear and limiting P.S. based statements.

Take a piece of paper and write down the following: I choose to easily, happily, and without limitation achieve _____ or more by _____ (date). Then just insert your goal and the deadline you've given it. Let's examine this and break it down further.

You are choosing your goal; it's not caused by chance. You are also choosing to achieve this *easily*; it shouldn't be hard. Notice that most people use the word "hard" when they talk about work. If you are moving steadily towards your goal and you are firm in your belief, then nothing about that has to be hard. No matter the effort, hours, or anything else, it does not have to be a challenge. Let's be real; digging ditches is hard. Selling is easy.

You are choosing to have no limitations. Sometimes you may achieve your goal, but in a different shape, size, or concept than you had originally imagined. It may even be much better than how you had initially conceived it. God, the universe, or what ever you believe in brought to you more than you could even consciously envision. Choose to receive without limitations. That's why I invite you to write down the ending phrase "or more." You will often receive more than you can conceive.

I believe in giving myself a deadline in order to put my brain, my body, and the universe in action. A goal without a deadline is often just an excuse to say, "maybe tomorrow." However, I do know that even if you choose your goal and the date by which you hope to accomplish it, you don't always achieve it by this time. It may come sooner, it may come later, and it may not come at all. But because you have set your actions in motion, you are poised to receive something bigger and better.

Once you have truly aligned the parts in your brain, you will free the space that is taken up with conflicting thoughts or ideas. Your goal has already been realized, even though you have not obtained it in a tangible form. I know that for many salespeople who are hardcore realists, the information in this chapter may be hard for you to swallow. All I invite you to do is to ask yourself if the competing messages in your brain are exactly the same as the "P.S. statements" I have talked about. Is it self-sabotage?

Looking to real-life examples of people who created their own success with the power of their minds is an inspirational way to see how this process can truly work. I have seen both, a movie about the billionaire mogul Howard Hughes and a TV biography about billionaire businessman Donald Trump. Both emphasized the importance of being able to train your brain and eliminate self-sabotage. Sales superstars tend to be competitive and almost maniacal in their desire to win. In the race to success, you discover the need to channel this energy toward your customer, and you must become intent upon with the idea of winning.

The movie *Aviator* depicted Howard Hughes' amazing ability to face any seemingly insurmountable obstacle, even those that his advisors deemed impossible. Hughes seemed to have an unconditional resolve to defeat any problem. His belief system was unbreakable, and void of any thought of failure. He was able to ignore so-called experts and others who continually told him that he was too deep in debt to finance his endeavors. Extreme risk never seemed to be intimidating to him. Howard Hughes had a belief system that allowed him to create his own destiny.

The biography of Donald Trump also portrayed a man with a sense of destiny. Most people judge his attitude as cocky or arrogant, but I see it as brilliance. Superstar performers in sports, sales, or any other endeavor have developed a belief system that supports and encourages them in their crusade for excellence.

Achieving superstar status in sales does not take a certain amount of education, money, experience, a good location, or any other restrictions that you may impose upon yourself. To achieve superstar results in sales simply takes one thing—the desire to do so. In other words, it takes passion. Passion will create the supportive belief system you need.

I have a saying—*"You are who you decide to be at any given moment."* Who you believe you are, is who you will become. At that moment, you have already achieved your desires—their date of fulfillment just has to be filled in. You must fake it until you make it. At the moment of that critical decision, you will have absolute faith in your destiny. Whenever your subconscious begins to generate negative thoughts as to why you can't do this, or how hard it will be, you must immediately catch these thoughts and destroy then. Identify and rewrite your P.S. statements. Create mental imagery of blasting that negative and limiting belief with a powerful weapon that annihilates it.

The more steps to success that you take, the more anecdotal evidence you have to solidify your positive and supporting belief system. You must use this evidence to create **RPMs—Recent Positive Moments** that give you momentum and support your changing belief system. Sales superstars create power in a belief system that supports their eventual triumph, no matter what temporary setbacks they might encounter. You must become what most people would describe as "delusional." A delusional mindset, contrary to popular belief, can be an absolutely healthy attribute in your progression toward your goals and sales profession. I believe that I am delusional in my mindset, but my delusion creates my reality. The power of knowing that your destiny is a choice is incredible. Sports announcer Al Michaels uttered the famous line, "Do you believe in miracles?" when the United States Olympic Hockey Team won the gold medal. Little did he know, the team already believed. Their beliefs helped them to create a winning destiny. What do *you* believe? Do you have the guts to create the delusional mind of a sales superstar? Or is your self-sabotaging subconscious already telling you that this is nuts, that it's okay not to believe in this, and that it's okay to just keep "working hard." The beauty is that it's your choice. So, what do *you* want to do? You will become whoever you believe you are, and you don't need anything "extra" that you may be telling yourself that you need. When people believe this, I call it the, **"When–Then Syndrome."** For example "When I get this, then I can do this;" or "When I accomplish this, then I will do this." Imagine your obstacles written on a dry erase board. Then simply erase them and take action.

Let Your Fantasy Be Your Reality

"In the mind of the beginner there are many possibilities and in the mind of the expert there are few."

—*Shunryu Suzuki, Teacher of Zen Buddhism*

What would you do in your sales career if you did not have limits? We know that everyone has self-imposed limits. They can stem from several strong forces—your environment, childhood experiences, workplace profiling, and other situations or experiences.

Your colleagues, clients, and supervisors continually judge you by what your strengths and weaknesses are, and what you can or cannot do. You must realize that all of these evaluations are subjective. Opinions of you are simply that—opinions. What someone thinks of you does not necessarily have anything to do with who you are, and you must never allow anyone to pigeonhole you into who you supposedly are or who you are not. The opinion that matters most is your own.

You can therefore use this opinion of yourself to create your own reality. You must continually feed your subconscious mind with the images and messages of who you want to be. Your subconscious does not reject any images or messages, so what you impress, you express. The dominant messages and images win out, whether they are good or bad. Further this by doing the following:

- Write down what you desire.
- Write it again and again until you can see it in your mind's eye.

- Picture yourself having achieved these goals, and doing the things you want to do.
- Don't let anyone detract from your mission.

Kids are a perfect group of people to look to for inspiration in achieving your goals. Kids are awesome, because they do not have years of built up fear, and have not come to accept a negative reality. They experience wonderment in most things. When my son Jake was five years old, he decided that he wanted to jump off the ten foot high diving board at the local YMCA swimming pool. Nearby adults who were with my wife were trying to caution her to stop him, so that he wouldn't get hurt. My wife didn't listen. Then when my son said that he was going to try to do a flip off the high diving board, the other adults went into cautioning overdrive, trying to communicate fear to both my wife and my son.

Despite the words of warning, Jake would not allow the fears of the adults to keep him from doing what he wanted. He tried to do the flip, and smacked the water hard. But then he tried again, and he kept trying until he did it right. Jake knew that he might not get it on the first try, but he also knew that this would not injure or kill him. He was willing to take action in the face of any fears he had. The other adults at the pool were not trying to keep him safe as much as they were trying to instill their own fears in him. But Jake ignored his own fears, and theirs as well and he did exactly what he said he was going to do. It is worth asking yourself, *"Would the child that you were be proud of the adult you have become?"*

Here is to never growing up.

3

Getting Your MBA—Massive Bank Account

The previous chapters laid down a lot of important ground work for your future sales success. You began the journey by truly embracing your sales career. You came to realize what mental roadblocks are currently denying you the level of success that you desire, and you figured out how to erase those roadblocks. Now you might be saying, "Great! Let's get to the magic sales skills that will give me all the sales success that I want." Not so fast—you have a lot more work to do before learning those skills can help you. I promised you a different kind of book on sales; one that would actually take you to superstar status. So let's do some more fundamental work first. In this chapter, I'll focus on success education.

When you read education did that make you cringe? I am not talking about attending a university (although there is nothing wrong with doing so). But formal education rarely equates to the type of knowledge you will need to succeed in sales. Unfortunately, I have seen many people with MBA degrees who couldn't function in the practical arena of business. Their accomplishments in academia did not translate to the real world. This is why we focus instead on *real world* sales education. To be a sales superstar, you must continually work on fundamentals. Let me give you a couple of good examples.

Every year during the first practice of the football season, legendary Green Bay Packers coach Vince Lombardi would say, "Gentleman, this is a football." Coach Lombardi started with the most basic element. As a great coach, he knew what I have come to discover; that at a certain point in their careers, people assume they have mastered things or know all that there is to know. To assume that is to make a mistake of losers. I have seen this many times in the veteran salesperson who rolls his eyes at the suggestion of further education, and retorts that he knows how to sell.

Retired basketball coach of the UCLA Bruins John Wooden took a similar approach, and kicked off practice every year explaining to his players how to put on their socks so they would not get blisters. On a TV program about Coach Wooden, one of his greatest all-time players Bill Walton told the story about his first practice. Walton said that after being one of the most actively recruited high school basketball players in history, he had arrived at UCLA anticipating the opportunity to witness the wisdom of a coach known as the "Wizard of Westwood." Coach Wooden began his first practice with his usual explanation about the socks and blisters. Walton recalled his shock at beginning his college basketball career with a lesson about how to put on socks, after he had been so awaiting Coach Wooden's first speech. When Walton asked his coach about what had just occurred, Wooden simply replied that he could teach Mr. Walton all about basketball, but if he had blisters and could not play because he had put his socks on wrong, then it would not matter how much he had learned.

I believe that the same is true for selling, and that both Coach Lombardi and Coach Wooden knew exactly what they were doing. You must set the stage to learn, and keep learning. You must start with the basics.

Education = Motivation

Great speaker, philosopher, entrepreneur, and mentor of mine, Jim Rohn has often told me of a long-running argument between himself and speaker/sales trainer Zig Ziglar. The argument, Mr. Rohn says, is over which comes first: motivation or education. Mr. Rohn says that Mr. Ziglar believes you have to get motivated first, while Mr. Rohn favors getting educated first. Mr. Rohn remarks that ". . . if you motivate someone and you don't educate them, then all you have is a motivated idiot." He's also stated that "A college education can get you a job, but self-education can make you rich."

I personally believe that motivation and education go hand in hand, and that education equals motivation. During my career motivating and educating salespeople, I have always found that when people learn something of value, they become extremely motivated. I have also found that during times when I have lost my usual level of motivation, my attitude can be traced directly back to a lack of commitment to my education.

I once had a friend tell me of a quote he saw on the wall of an IBM training center in Endicott, New York that said, *"There is never a saturation point to learning."* This has never been truer than it is today. The marketplace is currently changing at a more rapid rate than ever before in history. Technology is expanding almost exponentially; information for anything is easily available. The Internet has connected the world in ways that we could have never dreamed.

Computer processing speed has increased dramatically. This generates opportunities for technology to make things faster and easier, while creating new ways for salespeople and marketers to do their jobs. As an example of how fast things are changing, we look at Moore's Law, which is the empirical observation that the transistor density of integrated circuits doubles every 24 months. Essentially, this means that we are rapidly moving towards the age when processors will be able to somewhat duplicate human brain function. Technology, in and of itself, has changed the sales game. In 24 hours on the social networking web site MySpace.com, I can interact and form more connections than was ever possible in a year or more before this site was created. A salesperson can go online and in a day create almost completely automated follow-up and marketing campaigns. Those things would not have been possible a few years ago. With all of these processes becoming reality, how can it be possible for a person to not want to educate themselves extensively about these changes in order to ensure their success? It's simple—to become a superstar salesperson you must become and remain "on fire, with desire" for learning.

Education vs. Training

Let me make a distinction in the type of learning you must do versus the learning that will keep you from becoming a sales superstar. Another mentor of mine, Nido Quebin, President of High Point University in High Point, North Carolina, makes a distinction between training and education by using this analogy. If you had a child that you sent to school, would you rather your child get sex education or sex training? You might not want either—but being a father myself, I know I would prefer sex education. Sex education teaches about the subject, and sex training teaches how to do it. What good is the training if the person being trained is not educated about that which he or she being trained to do?

You might be saying, "But Mark, I don't get it. I want to know *how* to sell." Here is the difference between education and training: Traditional sales training focuses on what to do and how to do it. Education focuses on these things, but also tells you *why* you must do them. When the why becomes clear, the how becomes easy. Traditional selling approaches utilized selling systems or what's known as a *Road to the Sale*. While these systems or processes are very necessary and important, it is also imperative that you learn to think on your own. Gone are the days of having sales recruits learning only canned spiels and rehearsed closes.

Have you ever received a phone call from a telemarketer, or witnessed a salesperson read what is an obviously prepared script? How do they sound? How does it make you feel? Does it create a high sense of trust between you and that salesperson, and a sense of respect for their character? Not likely. Instead, you immediately want to hang up or run away. Those salespeople are a caricature of bad selling.

Am I telling you that you should never learn word tracks techniques or scripts? No, you absolutely should, and I will share some in this book. However, you must EDUCATE yourself as to why you are using these scripts, and what you are trying to accomplish with them. You must use what you learn and transform it in a personable way to be able to communicate and create trust.

There is an old phrase that states, "People buy from people." Notice that it does not say that people buy from *sales* people. People do business with those whom they know, trust, and probably like. Sales education focuses not only on the words but on the intent and desired outcome behind them. In other words, sales education concentrates on the "Why." It focuses on the customer rather than just what you should be saying to him. Traditional sales training tends to focus on how to react and reply; this type of sales training can move you towards manipulation rather than persuasion and cooperation. You must **TLC—Think Like a Customer.**

Many times over the years, I have been in the position of a customer, and have mystery shopped businesses on the phone. You can always spot salespeople who have been trained on a script. They sound like silly robots. It's almost as if they have to pause to turn the page. Whenever I come across these salespeople while mystery shopping, I notice that if I ask them a question, they often freak out; because a script doesn't allow for questions. Questions would even cause many of the salespeople to lose their spot in the script and begin to panic. I could practically hear them hyperventilating over the phone. I blame them *and* the silly sales manager that allowed this train wreck to happen.

If you are going to learn techniques, word tracks, scripts, closes, and objection responses, you had better know them inside and out, and you better know "why" you are using them. If any customer at any time asks you a question or has an objection, you had better know what to say and do *without having to think or blink.* Only when you are that much on top of your game will you exude confidence. The #1 reason why anyone buys anything is because of the confidence that the person selling it to them emanates. Always remember that *Competence = Confidence.*

Finding the Magic Learning Button

You gain and build the confidence necessary to sell successfully through education and practice. Let's go over exactly how you can educate yourself. There are three learning modalities—visual, auditory, and kinesthetic. Visual people tend to learn better by seeing or reading. Auditory people tend to learn better by listening. Kinesthetic people tend to learn better by doing, practicing, or mimicking. At this stage of your life, it's likely that you have had a lot of experience learning, and you should know which of these three ways you learn best. It all has to do with processing. Your brain tends to process information better in some ways than others. If you learn more effectively in a particular manner, don't fight it; just use it to your advantage.

You can increase your speed of education by utilizing the other modalities that come more naturally to you. Let me give you an example: I once was taking a snow skiing class. I was in a group of about eight skiers, and was the lone male skier (besides the instructor). The instructor would give verbal directions on skiing techniques, and then have us do what he had told us to do. The women in the group were doing well with the instructions, and I was doing horribly. (Imagine my embarrassment!)

Finally, a solution hit me. I told the instructor that I was much better at watching someone do something and mimicking their actions. I told him I was more of a visual and kinesthetic learner than an auditory learner. The instructor caught on to exactly what I was saying. From then on, he not only gave verbal instructions, but also tried harder to show me what he meant. I would follow behind him to mimic what he was trying to demonstrate. My success in learning from him increased dramatically and immediately. His readiness to teach me in the way in which I learned best made a world of difference. If educating yourself for sales success has alluded you, it may be chiefly from using the wrong modality.

As you learn techniques, word tracks, and closes, I invite you to be aware of your best learning modalities, and use them. For example, as a strong visual learner, I can learn quickly by reading, and I read between 75–100 books each year. I have taught myself to speed-read by utilizing instructional speed-reading books. Often, instead of speed reading,

I slow the process down by highlighting the key parts of the text. This combines the visual and kinesthetic learning modalities. I am a big believer in reading. Even for those of you who are auditory or kinesthetic learners, reading is key. If you become a habitual reader and take action on what you read, you will not be denied the success you desire.

"Read is the Root of Ready"

I cannot emphasize the "need to read" enough, in both business and in life. You can gain so much information from books. Remember, you must spend more time working on yourself than you do your job. When you get better, your sales will get better. I have read studies that say that the average person never reads another book after graduating from high school. I don't believe that you were put on this earth to waste your potential. I believe that you must make reading part of your regimen, even if it's not one the strongest ways that you learn. Your brain is indeed a muscle, so the more you use it, the stronger it will become. Reading will help even if it is one of your weaker learning modalities. Read books on self-development, sales, psychology, biographies, and every trade magazine you can find. You should absolutely scour and devour the trade magazines for your industry. You should be aware of every trend, vendor, and resource that is relevant to your business. Remember: "Readers are Leaders."

Reading will help you to become an expert in your field. Your customers want to do business with people who are experts and can share the information they need to solve their problems better than anyone else can. They want to feel like they have found the secret, hidden, and best resource. That resource should be you. Being that person for your customers takes thorough and continual self-education. You can use your education, expertise, and experience to inform others in your sales approach. This will help you to ask and inform versus "tell and sell."

Reading is ideal for visual learners; however, if you are a strong auditory learner, you can come up with other techniques to teach yourself the information you need. You can rehearse by recording what you need to learn, and then playing it back to yourself. Keep doing this over and over until you feel you have fully grasped what you are trying to learn. You may never "master" it, but you will reach a level of skill where you feel comfortable with this knowledge. To become a sales superstar, you must become good at listening and understanding your customer. If auditory learning is not your strongest method of learning, you will still have work on this modality to grow your abilities in this area. Although you may use the other areas in order to educate yourself, your customers will often attempt to express their needs to you through verbal delivery. When a customer is telling or explaining things to you, you must be able to process the information. Losing sales because you are weak in auditory processing is not acceptable. The auditory modality is one area all salespeople must become good or even great at.

Sometimes it's necessary to use more than one learning modality in order to really teach yourself something well. For several years, I recorded a lot of shows for a satellite television education network. I would fly into Texas and go to their studios to tape up to 25 thirty-minute shows, often in only a day or two. Occasionally, I would also tape shorter, five-minute segments. During my years doing these shows, I rarely had to record a second take, no matter how many shows I did in a row. (For any of you who might have done TV or radio, you know this can be difficult and quite draining!) The reason that I think I was able to do so many shows successfully and in only one take was my self-education regimen. I taught myself the information using the following process:

1st – I would write out my shows.

2nd – I would rewrite them until I felt like they were a part of my subconscious mind.

3rd – I would record the shows while performing them in front of a mirror. I would then rerecord, and keep doing so until I had it down cold and felt that my performance was excellent.

4th – I would listen to the recording over and over—while I exercised, while I ate, while I relaxed on the deck. I listened to it repeatedly on my headphones on the plane ride to Texas to tape the shows, and I would listen in the hotel room the night before.

By doing this, I made the recordings a part of my brain. Often, I would not even use teleprompters while taping, because I didn't need them. The shows weren't "canned," but they were well rehearsed, natural, and had become second nature to me. If at any time later in the day I felt that I was getting fatigued or momentarily lost during the taping, I didn't panic. I took a deep breath and let the part of my mind that knew the show by heart take over. Almost always, my brain would bring exactly what I needed to the forefront.

You must create a groove in your brain with what you want to learn. You must analyze it and reanalyze it so that you are educating instead of training yourself. Training is short-term, while education becomes a part of every fiber of your being. I believe that training is like getting a sunburn. It burns and then it fades away. Education is permanent.

Group Education—Learning with Others

No matter what product or service you sell, you will notice quickly that all the objections to it tend to fall into a few specific categories, and that there are really just a few objections in each category. You can help identify these objections by taking the time at the end of every day to do a review. Imagine the sales sequence that you are replaying in your brain as a football game. After a game, the coaches review the game film and break down every play of the game. They critique each effort and define how to improve their team's performance. In the same way, you must review each contact and selling effort you made that day. "Replay" everything in your head. What happened from beginning to end? Specifically:

- How did you greet the customer? What was your opening?
- How did the customer reply? What questions did he ask?
- How did you reply to his questions?
- What were his objections to your answers?
- How did you reply to his objections?

- What happened after the objection was stated?
- Do you believe that all of the decision makers relevant to the call were present?
- If not, could you have done something differently to involve all the decision makers up front?
- Did you offer any alternatives to the customer?
- Did you make a presentation/demonstration or did you just simply tell the customer about what you are selling?
- Did you make a proposal to the customer?
- Did you find the customers' keyword hot buttons?
- Did you tap into the emotions the customer was seeking by obtaining the product or service?

Imagine if you, your sales team members, and sales managers went into a meeting room and you did the above exercise with each sales representative for each sales contact made the day before. You collectively looked at the contacts, what happened, and what possibly could have been done differently or better. Everyone's brains are focusing intently on improving the process for future contacts. If you are together in a physical location, you can write down all the pertinent facts about the deal on a board and interact visually, auditory, and by writing them on a board (kinesthetic) and then discussing them (auditory). If you are in different locations, you can use a webinar to do the same thing.

You will be amazed at how much you can improve, and help each other improve, by opening your mind to all possibilities. In sales, you cannot afford to live in a vacuum. If you constantly make the same mistakes over and over without reviewing and improving, you are committing career suicide. You need others' input to aid in educating yourself; and in turn, you will help to educate them as well.

Even if you cannot get a team of salespeople together, you can get your manager or another sales associate to become your sales partner. Every salesperson should have a sales partner who can assist the other in improving his sales skills. I would recommend role-playing for fifteen minutes a day with your partner on three to six common objections that your customers bring forth. Next, I would take your most recent unsuccessful contacts, and swap them with your sales partner. You should get in touch with each others' contacts, and say something like this:

"Hi, my name is Mark Tewart. I am a sales and customer service representative from ABC Company. Real quickly Mr. Jones, the reason for my call is that I noticed from our records that you were visiting with a representative from our company recently, and I am following up because I want to find out how everything went. Who was your representative, by the way?" (See if the customer remembers the salesperson.) *"Did you have any further questions? Mr. Jones, just being curious, if I were to ask you to pick just one reason why you did not make the decision to purchase the product/service so far, what would that one reason be?"*

Now that you have flushed out objections, you can work towards trying to give the customer **HFG—Hope for Gain** to further the sale.

Notice that you are accomplishing two things here: (1) You are taking a TO (Turnover) on an unsold customer to maximize all contacts; and (2) You are learning from what the customer tells your sales partner. If a customer did not feel good about you, and if they did not tell you their real objection, it may be hard for them to be honest with you on the phone. If your sales partner calls, they hear a different voice, and the customer can now do what we call in sales, "save face."

Another way to learn from one another is for you and your sales partner to each choose one book that could help your sales career, read a chapter each within a specified time, and then report to one another what you've learned. You can greatly enhance your learning exponentially, create accountability, and add some fun. Your goal should be to include books, CD's, downloads, seminars, webinars, teleseminars, CD-ROMs, mentoring, and as many other media as possible.

Successful People Mastermind with Others. So Why Do Only a Few Do it?

If you read biographies of successful people you will often find a common theme: They all tend to have mentors who teach them individually, and they surround themselves with groups of successful people to learn from and share information.

Most salespeople, even good ones, tend to isolate themselves and avoid seeking the help of others. Many become comfortable being average, rather than trying to find mentors and masterminds. Most salespeople tell themselves they can't afford to solicit input or education from others. They often make excuses as to why they don't have the time to go to seminars or meetings. Sometimes even *good* salespeople are reluctant to pursue information from others because their ego and arrogance hold them back. They think that they know what they are doing, and that's enough. Many salespeople think that educators and mentors who sell instruction and information are just trying to make a buck. They claim that "those who can, do—and those who can't, teach."

Notice that I didn't use the term "superstar salespeople" in any of these descriptions. Sales superstars know that they have to educate themselves continually to get to the top and stay there. Sales superstars may have huge egos, but they keep them in check when it comes to getting education. They know that there are always people out there who have more knowledge than they do, and they never stop looking for these people and for other sources of the information that may help them. Sales superstars have what my friend and business associate Paul Chinian calls "a teachable spirit."

Superstar salespeople know that you must surround yourself with the best in your industry, and form a mastermind circle. This is certainly not a new concept, but it is one of the most effective. You cannot surround yourself with losers and become a sales superstar. You must cut out the cancer. To this end, at the close of every year, you should write down the names of all the negative and cancerous people that you know. You should then make a plan to eliminate them from your life, and you should do the same for all negative, cancerous, and unsupportive activities and habits in your life. Cut out cancer before it grows.

In addition to same-industry mastermind circles, you should also form non-industry mastermind circles with members from other industries by doing the following:

Call the largest real estate agency in town, and ask to speak to their number one salesperson. When that salesperson takes the call, introduce yourself, and say that you have heard that he or she is the best salesperson for their agency. Tell the salesperson that you're calling because you are a salesperson in another industry, and that you would be honored to buy his or her breakfast, lunch, or dinner if you could just pick his or her brain for 30 minutes. Promise them that you will not be a pest, that you have done your homework, and that you have some specific questions you would like to ask. Let the agent know that you value his or her expertise, experience, and results, and would be privileged to listen to their ideas. Offer to pay the agent for their time, if need be.

Once you have met with the person, see if they would be interested in helping you create a mastermind circle with people from other industries that are top-notch salespeople. Form your own mastermind group, and use it to learn from the best. I believe you can learn as much or possibly more from mastermind circles that include participants from different industries as you can from groups that include only people from your own industry.

Unfortunately, mastermind circles from within your own industry can tend to overuse and generalize information and ideas. What's often being shared is the same old regurgitated garbage from twenty years prior. I have witnessed this time and time again in the auto industry, in what is known as "Dealer Twenty Groups." These groups are made up of roughly twenty different auto dealers, usually of the same brand(s) and approximate size. Outdated, traditional advertising campaigns are shared, numbers are shared, excuses are given for a lack of results, and often, nothing is accomplished.

To avoid falling into such a trap, find out from a manufacturer, association, or industry trade magazine editors who the top sales performers in your industry are. Call these sales superstars in other parts of the country, tell them how you got their names, and let them know that you heard they were the best in the industry. Tell them that because they are in another region, you will not be competing with them for business—you are calling because you appreciate and want to be able to duplicate their success. Let them know that you realize they are busy, and that you respect their time. Tell them that you would be honored if you could ask them just a few questions to uncover the secrets to their success, and that you would be willing to pay them for this or return the favor in any way that you can.

Potential mentors and mastermind groups are abundant. You have to remain humble and condition yourself to recognize them when you see them. Whenever I hear the term "self made," I cringe. *There is no such thing as self-made success.* Everyone is the sum of many parts that are made up of many people, experiences, and education. You must remain open to these people, experiences, and education to continue to grow as a superstar salesperson.

Educating Through Experience: Mystery Shop

I think that everyone in sales should periodically check out your competition by mystery shopping. If nothing else, you will probably find out what *not* to do as much as what to do. It becomes painfully obvious how bad and amateurish your so-called competition is. The good news is that, in the field of selling, often your competition is so bad that you're able to learn from their mistakes to hone and improve your own skills.

The Bottom Line is that Most Salespeople Suck!

By mystery shopping your competition via phone, email, web, or in person, you can quickly see things from a customer's perspective. You will instantly understand what I mean and why I advocate the **Contrarian Sales Approach.** This approach will allow you to stand out from the competition by selling in the opposite way that they do. During your mystery shopping, rate your competition on everything, including accessibility, friendliness, voice tone, presentation, demonstration, problem solving, alternatives, and offers.

During my years as general manager of an automobile dealership, we often advocated that our new hires mystery shop other car dealerships to get a sense of what was going on with the competition. Even new salespeople would come back amazed at the lack of care and skills that were displayed. It gave them a sense of hope and encouragement, that even as new employees, they could do well. They just had to remember that they could never assume they knew everything about selling, and always had to be ready and willing to learn more.

There was one instance where the manufacturer for our automobile dealership hired a consultant to mystery shop dealerships of our brand in our area. The consultant was to report back to the manufacturer all of his experiences—both good and bad—while shopping at the dealerships. He came to our dealership posing as a customer, and brought along his girlfriend as part of the decoy. We wound up selling his girlfriend a vehicle. The consultant later described us as the "Saks Fifth Avenue of Car Dealers," and used his experience with us to improve his own practice. He learned something from us, and he met professional salespeople. By mystery shopping yourself, you can compare your experiences with good *and* bad salespeople, and contrast how each does business.

Over the years and in my experience as a consultant, speaker, and expert in the automotive industry, I have shopped for a vehicle at dealerships hoping not to be recognized. I remember one instance where my wife and I visited a Midwestern BMW dealership. We had just worked out, and were in our gym clothes. It was probably during the last couple of hours that the dealership was open on a holiday weekend. We drove up in a non-expensive vehicle.

It became immediately obvious to us that these factors—our exercise clothes, arrival around closing time and on a holiday, and driving a less-than-luxury automobile—caused the salespeople at the dealership to pre-judge and neglect waiting on us. We finally cornered a salesperson and asked about a vehicle. The salesperson acted annoyed. We asked to test drive the vehicle, and the salesperson responded by grumbling something about it being within an hour of closing. He then threw us the keys and told us to take the car ourselves, because he didn't want to get beat up by the wind in a convertible. During our test drive, there was a problem with the performance. We found out later that the issue was something minor that could have been easily explained—if the salesperson had been doing his job and been with us on the test drive. However, he was not.

When my wife and I arrived back at the dealership, I gave the salesperson the keys and thanked him. He never asked for my name, contact information, or if I was interested. However, as we were leaving, he asked where we lived. When I answered him, he recognized our neighborhood as an affluent area. Suddenly, he became interested. TOO LATE! This salesperson had lost us as potential customers because of his decision to not treat us as customers from the beginning. A tremendous amount of sales are lost everyday because many salespeople are pre-judging or over-qualifying customers to the point that they don't even attempt to *make* a sale in the first place. There is one thing that is certain: If you don't attempt the sale, you can't make a sale. As great hockey player Wayne Gretzky said, "You miss 100 percent of the shots you don't take."

This experience and others have always led me to encourage sales-people to mystery shop. You may be saying, "Sure, but Mark, this was a car dealership, and they are horrible." Don't kid yourself; I can give you horror stories from experiences with real estate, insurance, retail, manufacturers, and almost any other field you can think of. Mystery shopping will overwhelm you with education and will truly wake you up to the caliber of business that is done on a daily basis. If you are lucky, you will witness a great salesperson and have a good experience; but always keep in mind that you can learn something from both.

Tap Into the Brains of Experts

The Internet allows anyone anywhere to immediately obtain information about whatever they want. There are enough free resources on the web to keep you busy learning for life. Join free blogs, RSS feeders, and email newsletters. Using these resources will allow you to obtain valuable information and be exposed to a "who's who" of resources. You will find that with a little effort, it's not hard to connect with just about any of these people. Remember, when you contact someone you must try to make it mutually rewarding and not waste his or her time. Remain humble, but show that you are a student who is willing and eager to learn.

Several years ago when I was beginning my career as a professional speaker, I reached out to the late Dottie Walters. Dottie is a legend in the speaking industry. She was a speaker, owner of one of the largest speakers' bureaus in the world, and was regarded for having written the best-selling speaking book of all time, "Speak and Grow Rich" (Prentice Hall, 1997). I was introduced to Dottie at my first National Speakers Association meeting, and we spoke for just a minute. Several weeks after the meeting, I called her at her office. I told her I had some specific questions for her, and that I knew that she was very busy. However, if she could take some time to briefly assist me, I would be willing to help her out in any way that she saw fit when she next spoke in my area.

I will never forget how Dottie spent an hour with me on the phone, and the invaluable advice that she gave me. She later mailed and faxed me relevant and useful resources for free. She really didn't know me from Adam, but was willing to assist in some way. On the phone, at seminars, and through email and blogs, I have reached out to other people such as Jim Rohn, Mark Victor Hanson, Dan Kennedy, and Nido Qubein (just to name a few). Although these experts were busy and had limited time to assist me, they all did. Go out of your way to offer these experts assistance—volunteer work, free rides, or anything else that would show your appreciation for their readiness to share their knowledge with you.

Over the years, I have tried to "pay it forward" myself, and help people who are looking for advice from someone in my field. I have spent countless hours with people "on fire with desire" to be salespeople, speakers, and entrepreneurs. I am always impressed most with the people who understand the proposition of sales, and use it in their conversations with me. Offer to give something first, even if the person to whom you are reaching out does not accept it. Such effort shows your determination. Never ask for anything for free without offering to pay in some way as well. These experts are not Socialist resources for you advancement; however, they are people from whom you can, and should, best learn about your industry.

Success Metrics—Measure Twice, Cut Once

"A person who won't do the small things can't be trusted to do the big things."

– Unknown

I may be the least handy person on earth. I am the antithesis of the "do-it-yourselfer." However, I take the phrase "Measure twice, cut once" to heart. In some respects, I apply that to selling. You should measure everything you do.

In many seminars and training classes over the years, I have asked salespeople to give me specific sales production numbers. I have asked the salespeople their sales average, average margins, or gross profits. I've asked how many customer contacts and follow-up calls they make a month, how many emails they send, and what their closing ratios, average commissions, customer retention averages, and referral numbers are.

Here is what I've discovered: Superstars measure everything, average salespeople "guesstimate," and poor salespeople wing it without quantifying anything. Superstars usually know to the percent, the dollar, or the odd number, all of their results. Although many sales superstars are not detail-oriented by nature, it's amazing how detailed they become when it comes to money.

> "If you don't know where you are at, how can you know how to get where you are going?"
>
> – *Mark Tewart*

You should always measure your actions and your results. It does not do a baseball player any good to know he has 100 hits if he does not know how many times he has been to bat. There are a gazillion software programs, daily planners, and other tools that can help you measure all that you do. Pick one you like and use it regularly.

If you are a business owner and you mail out 100 letters with a specific offer, and you can't measure the results, then you are throwing money down the drain. Such mistakes occur every day with businesses and salespeople. You must measure, measure, measure, by using the following parameters:

- How many phone calls did you make?
- How many appointments did you get?
- How many presentations did you make?

- How many deals closed?
- How many set 2nd appointments?
- How many phone calls did you take?
- How many appointments were made and kept?
- What is your be-back ratio?
- What is your average commission?

I invite you to work backwards. Let's use the following example:

- $20,000 monthly commissions
- $500 average commission
- 40 sales
- At a 25 percent closing ratio you would need 160 customer contacts to close 40 deals. I would even build in a fail factor of 10 to 20 percent. So you would need to see 176–192 customers.
- In 20 working days you would need between 8.8–9.2 customer contacts per day.
- How many sales will come from prospecting, advertising, referrals, or repeats?
- What will increase your margin and closing ratios to reach your goal sooner?
- What will bring you more customer contacts in an automated or semi-automated fashion?

Measure, Measure—and Then Ask How You Can Improve Each Step

When I was in middle school, my brother Gary gave me a book titled, *Psycho-Cybernetics* by Maxwell Maltz (Prentice Hall, 1960). This is a self-improvement book that shares ways in which you can program and reprogram your mind. At my age and for that time, it was pretty heady stuff. The book had a major impact on me, and I was able to feel immediate results by utilizing teachings from it.

Throughout my entire life, I have experienced and witnessed the incredible results that occur as a result of self-education and self-improvement.

I have been a student and a teacher of success and sales superstars. I have attended several hundred seminars, read tons of books, listened to countless CD's, been involved in a variety of mastermind groups, sought out experts, and studied others from afar. A common theme among superstars is never-ending self-education, development, and improvement.

4

Getting What You Want Right Now!

Why Traditional Goal-Setting Keeps You Broke

Every year in January, gyms and health clubs are packed with determined people that have the good intention to go for their goals and New Year's resolutions. Everyone stands in line waiting to use the equipment, and the work-out classes are fully booked. The exercisers in the gym trying to achieve their goals and resolutions all have very determined looks on their faces. But by March, 95 percent or more of those originally determined people have given up. What happened to their determination? Why did they quit? How does their quitting affect future goals they may set? When people give up, it creates a mental and emotional anchor for the expectation and acceptance of failure. Traditional goal-setting sounds good in theory, and makes you feel good momentarily; but it does not get the job done. To accomplish your goals, you must understand your patterns and take intelligent, quantifiable action.

Goal-setting, as you've known it until now, involves a declaration of desire. Unfortunately, this desire is usually stated in a way that reinforces the negative. Traditional goal-setting can also limit your view of what you really want. Some examples are: "I want to get out of debt," "I want to pay my bills," "increase sales," "make more money," "be the top salesperson," "stop smoking," and "begin exercising."

When a person says they want to get out of debt, for example, they are stating what they want to get away from, instead of what they want to move towards. Usually people will state the goal in the form of a need, as in, "I *need* to get out of debt." Stating your goal in this way tends to reinforce the pain of your current situation. Pain is powerful emotion, and it often serves as an anchor that ties you to the very state of thinking and emotions that create it in the first place. Expressing need reinforces that you are needy, and needy people don't get what they want.

The following is a typical pattern: You focus on your needs, and then, through the goals that you've set based on these needs, you temporarily move away from the pain that the needs create. Pain can be an incredible motivator. However, without moving the focus away from the pain towards the desired end result, you add force to all of the emotion, imagery, and patterns that pull you right back into what had initially caused your pain. For example, instead of stating, "I am in debt, and I need to get out," try stating the following: "I am earning _____ dollars and I am living abundantly and debt free." Focus on the solution, instead of on the problem itself. Restating your problem only emphasizes it and creates negative emotional and mental anchors to it.

Now consider some other examples—increasing sales, making more money, being a top salesperson, or beginning an exercise regimen. These intentions are good, but as goals, they are missing several key points. First, you must decide *why* you want something. Remember, when the why gets strong, the how gets easy. Words are cheap. It's easy to say you want something; but you must uncover what is behind this desire. Second, you must proclaim your goal in present tense, not simply as something that you *want,* but as something that you already have or are currently experiencing. "I am the top salesperson selling ____ (number or dollars and volume of) _____." or, "I am exercising for _____ (minutes) _____ (times) a week." Proclaiming your goals in this way makes them feel as though they are reality, which brings you one step closer to *making* them reality.

Creating a Clear Vision

In Chapter 2, I discussed how to express your goals in a sentence form that makes your goal a choice. Once you have made these choices and declared your goals in the present tense as though you have achieved them, you can begin to move forward. You can move yourself mentally and emotionally from desire and need and truly see yourself accomplishing your goals.

The ability to see your goals being realized in what I call your "mind's eye" is critical. Once you have written your goal and can picture it clearly, you must write it indelibly in your brain through repetition. Write the sentence twenty, fifty, or even one hundred times per day. You might read this and think, "Is that really necessary?" Well, it depends on how badly you really want to achieve the goal. Like someone who asks if they have to practice something every day; the answer is, no, only on the days you want to succeed.

It's good to know your goal, and to repetitively anchor the goal into your conscious and subconscious mind; but let's add some steps to make sure that you reach the goal. Try to discern some positive patterns in your personal history, and discuss how you can use those patterns to accomplish your current goals. Then, add some actionable ideas to accomplish your goals. Here's the plan:

1. Discover and leverage your previous and existing positive imagery and emotions.
2. Create powerful statements of intention.
3. Take actions on your goal.
4. Reinforce the action until completion of the goal.

As you think about and review your life, do the following:

First, identify the successes you have had in your life. Write down both big and small achievements.

Next, try to identify the patterns that may have led to or been an integral part of your successes. See the accomplishments in your mind's eye in as vivid detail as possible, and feel the emotions that they incited as strongly as you can feel them. Anchor these thoughts and feelings of success into your brain and body.

I have personally experienced how potent the power of envisioning your own success can be. Let me give you an example from my middle school days. I attended a basketball camp where one of our guest instructors was a free throw expert. The instructor worked with college and professional basketball players on their free-throw shooting. The instructor divided my fellow campers and I into small groups. Each one of us had to shoot ten free throws as he recorded our results. The guest instructor then coached us on the proper mechanics of shooting free throws. He then had us close our eyes, and in slow motion, physically mimic shooting free throws without the ball. As we went through the motions, we were told to envision the ball swishing into the basket, hitting nothing but net. We did this exercise over and over for several minutes.

The instructor then told us to open our eyes, and when we did, we could see that he was holding a full size goal and backboard, that had been on the ground, upright. The instructor took out a nickel, and placed the nickel at the front of the room. He told us to look at the nickel, and to use it as our visual goal.

We then closed our eyes again, and the instructor directed us to envision the nickel. He told us to concentrate intently on it, and to see it on the rim of a basket that was now twice the size that it has been before. The instructor told us to visualize ourselves going through the proper mechanics of shooting a free throw. He asked us to picture the ball being released from our fingers, as we were pronating our wrist and following through, while still concentrating on the nickel. "Look at the nickel instead of the ball," he said. "Keep your eye on the nickel." He then told us to see the ball coming into view at the top of rim, and moving slowly over the nickel into the net. SWISH!

After doing this drill in slow motion for several minutes, he had us open our eyes again. One by one, we lined up at the free throw line and shot ten free throws while he once again recorded the results. A large majority of the campers improved their results from the first ten free throws. Many of the campers improved dramatically. These strong improvements came relatively quickly and perhaps most amazingly, *without physically shooting* one practice free throw. They were the result of setting a goal, creating a path to get there, and then visually imprinting the process into our brains with positive results. Although I had already believed that it was possible to accomplish goals through the power of positive thinking, this experience had just given me undeniable proof.

Now, try the following exercise to help you envision your own success in an equally powerful way: Write 100 goals in as few words as possible. Don't over think this; just write. There are no restrictions. You may actually have a hard time thinking of 100 goals. It might help you to think with the mind of a child, using that "anything is possible" outlook that I discussed at the end of Chapter 2. If you asked a young child to come up with 100 things they wanted for Christmas, they could probably do it at warp speed. The difference between children and most adults is that adults have become "mature"—a word that I personally dislike. Maturity is often nothing more than an excuse to lose your dreams and undermine your ability to reach them. Adults live with filters—their own, and others. They become myopic in their views. My word of caution is that you never allow the filters of others to contaminate your vision and limit your goals. Forget the naysayers; they don't pay your mortgage! It reminds of an old quote—*90 percent of people don't care about your problems and the other 10 percent are glad you have them.*

This type of rapid goal-setting—your "Christmas wish list" of goals—is an exercise that can help you to pull back blinders and filters, and get you excited. Creating sales superstardom is about generating and welcoming realities that you would have never before thought were possible. Write down both short and long-term goals. It's natural to have more short-term than long-term goals, and having a lot of short-term goals allows you to gain momentum and experience victory. This success will give you **RPM—Recent Positive Momentum.** As the gas pedal does in a vehicle, RPMs are experiences that give you forward momentum. These events create positive mental and emotional anchors that will guide you in the creation and accomplishment of your goals.

To increase your RPM, do the following:

- Write down your 90-day goals in addition to your longer-term goal list. Life seems to move in cycles and seasons—spring, summer, fall, winter, and for me, football. You have likely experienced significant differences and mood swings in your life in just a short period, such as a month or a season. A lot can be accomplished in just 90 days, and 90-day goal-setting brings reality and possibility to your goals, because you are focusing on the short-term future. You can envision the short-term goals being accomplished much easier than you can a long-term goal, which takes more action and faith.

- After you write your goals, write down seven things that can help you achieve your vision. What are the things you can do, see, acquire, or use to help you reach your goals? Specifically—are there places you can go, classes you can take, or books you can read? Is there particular research or information-gathering that you should be engaging in?

- Next, list seven people who can help you achieve your vision. They do not have to be people you know; they can be anyone in the world who can assist you in your achievements. In the age of the Internet, you are only a few people away from reaching anyone with whom you wish to connect. It's kind of like a goal-setting version of the trivia game, "Six Degrees of Kevin Bacon." The world is much smaller and much more accessible than you might think it is.

- Use rewards as you take the little steps necessary in meeting your goals—gathering information, going places you need to visit, speaking with people who can help you. Everyone needs rewards and positive reinforcement. Write down the compensation you will give yourself when you accomplish the goal. Also, write down how you will reward yourself as you move towards your goal. There isn't a law that says you shouldn't be rewarded every day. If you break everything down into small segments, you will see that everything is indeed doable.

- Write down your greatest skills, talents, and attributes. What do people compliment you on? What talents have you shown? What things come naturally to you that may be difficult for other people? Fill in the blank here: "I experience excellence when I ____." Talent is God-given, and skills are learned. Often, people don't recognize their talents, or sometimes they downplay them. Recognizing and accepting your talents can be a powerful step towards reaching your goals.

Seeing Yourself Successful—A Few More Visualizing Techniques

Picture Your Dream Day, Dream Week, and Dream Life – If you could picture your perfect day, what would it look like to you? How would you spend each hour of your "dream day?" Would your day consist of work, play, or both? What would you be experiencing? How would you feel? Can you see the colors? Can you hear the sounds? What do you smell? When you finish envisioning and writing about your dream day, then write about your dream week, day-by-day. Then take the exercise a step further, and write your dream life. What would you be doing? What would your house look like? What kind of vehicle would you drive? What relationships would you have? What would your mental, spiritual, physical, and emotional life be like?

100th Birthday Interview – Imagine that you are 100 years old, and that someone is interviewing you about your life. Picture yourself talking about what had occurred over the years. What accomplishments would you have achieved? What relationships would you have formed? Who had you mentored or helped? Where would you have traveled? What would be your legacy?

Usually, when you set goals, you are looking forward. This exercise allows you to start at the end, and look backwards, and gain a different and hopefully clearer perspective about what you may want.

Daily Habits – Write down the specific daily habits that you need to undertake in order to reach your goals; some of the following are examples:

1. Exercise for one hour per day to have strength and energy
2. Spend time praying and seeking spiritual guidance
3. Communicate with mentors
4. Spend time and talk with family
5. Eat healthy food, and drink lots of water

6. Educate myself
7. Market my business for one hour per day and create automated marketing for conquest customers and existing customers
8. Set career goals, update goals, and visualize my accomplishments
9. Set up and review my specific customer retention program
10. Make (insert number) __ customer contacts
11. Set (insert number)__ appointments

Try to set and live your "success habits." Success is like a muscle; a little bit of effort every day helps to build it.

Some people may consider these exercises silly. If this is your take, then consider the following: Can anyone deny the power of the "placebo effect?" It's been proven in many different medical studies that giving someone a sugar pill that they believe is medicine, often produces the same positive results experienced by those who have received the real medicine. Have you ever worried about the possibility of getting sick, and shortly thereafter, actually did get sick? Is that just a coincidence; or is that a thought manifesting itself?

Optimism does not have to be blind to reality in order to be effective. You can be an optimist, and even have the positive, delusional belief system that I have discussed previously; but deal in real, daily actions that move you closer towards any goal you desire. Your positive belief system supports your actions, even in moments of fear and weakness. Superstar salespeople are definitely optimists, and not cynics. In fact, there is a famous joke about the optimism of salespeople. The world was coming to an end. *The New York Times* headline read "The End," and the *Los Angeles Times* headline read "Doomsday is Near." However, the salesperson trade journal read "The End is Near, Salespeople Optimistic." Even in the worst of situations, salespeople are known for remaining positive.

The Power of Now

I am fairly certain that every trainer or speaker you have ever listened to has talked about the power of goals. You have heard over and over about how to look toward what you want, and *then* figure out how to get it.

Unfortunately, you have been duped. Traditional goal-setting doesn't work, and it certainly doesn't work quickly. However, there is a way to get what you want, and get it right now.

Although you may think that I've lost my mind, let me explain. The intention of conventional goal-setting is to look toward the future, and to plan for what you desire. Goals provide hope. Remember from Chapter 1 that my definition of hope is, **H**aving **O**ptimistic **P**redictions & **E**motions. However, traditional goal-setting can create the biggest stumbling block to actually getting what you desire as quickly as you can. This method focuses on taking distinct, chronological steps in order to reach your goals, or doing what is known as "climbing the ladder to success." Achieving what you want by taking things one step at a time is a common course of action. I invite you to be contrarian in your thinking and to break the rules by jumping to the top rung of the ladder. Instead of taking one step at a time, try taking a giant leap. Don't listen to the dogma of *paying your dues*; instead, know that you are worthy of achieving what you desire right now. Believing that your goals can be achieved rapidly allows you to take a major step towards breaking the chains of conventional thought—chains that can hold you back from being a sales superstar, and being one right now.

Ralph Waldo Emerson said, *"The only thing that will grow is that which you give energy to."* To focus your mind on what you desire is an important step. However, most people immediately begin to try to figure out *how* they can accomplish their goal. This line of questioning often leads to fear and over-emphasis of logic. Fear and logic cause people to concentrate on all of the potential barriers, which they then begin to see as *actual* barriers. These barriers either delay results or completely keep you from getting what you want. Instead of asking "how," concentrate on *why* you want something. I keep coming back to this concept of knowing the reasons for your goals, because when you are clear on the why, figuring out how will become clear. Asking yourself why you want something gets you in touch with your thoughts and emotions, which in turn attract the answers. It's much easier to attract something naturally and immediately than to chase after something and push it away due to the fear that it will be scarce or elusive. In fact, these ideas are supported by a concept called the Law of Attraction.

Let's discuss the Law of Attraction and how it applies to your goals. Wikipedia gives the following definition for the Law of Attraction:

The phrase **Law of Attraction** has been used by many esoteric writers, although the actual definition varies greatly. Most authors associate the Law of Attraction with a theory that "like attracts like," usually as applied to the mental life of human beings: that individuals experience physical and mental manifestations corresponding to their predominant thoughts, feelings, words, and actions; and that they thereby have the ability to control the reality of their lives through thought alone. The principle is based on the concept that a person's thoughts (conscious and unconscious), emotions, beliefs, and actions attract corresponding positive or negative experiences. This process has been described as "harmonious vibrations of the law of attraction," or "you get what you think about; your thoughts determine your experience."

In other words, your thoughts are impressed into your subconscious mind; or, as Mark Victor Hansen says, *"What you impress, you express."* All of your thoughts and actions will attract similar thoughts and actions from people and events that will support your original patterns. The Law of Attraction is a universal law of nature supported by metaphysics and quantum physics. The ideas that I've expressed about envisioning and attracting your own goals, therefore, are not just my own notions; they are theories supported by science that can be applied to everyday life.

The failure in goal-setting takes place when someone tries to go out of their way to get something, rather than naturally attracting it. People constantly use terms like "hard work" to describe their goal-achieving process. Obstacles arise when someone tries to figure out *how* to get something rather than determine *why* they want it. This creates subconscious struggles and messages of difficulty. Even someone with the best of intentions quickly tires of this struggle and quits entirely. This failure establishes a pattern that is rooted in the subconscious as evidence of strain, frustration, and disappointment. Reasons to lower standards or to simply give up become stronger than reality. But true power comes from knowing that *"You are who you decide to be at any given moment."* It doesn't require jumping over any hurdles; it only takes resolving to be and to have what you wish for. By doing this and thereby eliminating the 'how-to' hurdles as obstacles, you can begin to think about, act on, and attract your desires. You may not know exactly how and when this is occurring, but you must trust that it is.

The root of the word "decide" is from the Latin word "*decidere*," and literally means "to cut off." Thus, to decide is to cut yourself off from all other possibilities. The power of this intention will create a different belief system that will elevate your actions to a much higher level. People who succeed and obtain their goals regularly simply operate at higher levels of consciousness than people who do not.

The problem that arises when you set goals without understanding the power and process of your mind is that you often create the exact opposite of what you desire. You establish objectives that focus on solving a problem and you therefore, as we have come to discover, end up concentrating on what you *don't* want to happen. This focus feeds the negative energy which, according to the Law of Attraction, will draw towards you the people, things, or events that match that negative energy. You have amplified and multiplied the problem, instead of fixing it. Such self-sabotage is the underlying reason for a lot of your struggles, conflicts, and limitations. To eliminate self-sabotage and truly get what you desire, you must first desire, then understand why you desire, and finally, trust in your desire. To do all of this effectively, you must learn to relax; because when you are stressed out, your thoughts, emotions, inner dialogue, and the ensuing actions serve as a distraction from your desires. Stress focuses the mind on other things and renders you powerless to receive the answers that may be right in front of you.

The secret to getting what you want is realizing the power of now. The future is determined when you realize and truly accept that your desires can be created and cultivated at this very moment, and when you decide, accept, and act with the power of now.

Do you Believe in Santa Claus?

My son Jake still believes in Santa Claus. It's a blast to watch him believe in something that's so much fun for him. There are no limitations to what

Jake believes you can ask for and believe in. As an adult, do you believe the same things? You should, because you are, in essence, your own Santa Claus. You get to decide what you get and what you don't. As adults, we tend to forget this, and we become conditioned to accept "reality" and "maturity" as factors that are out of our control. Don't let your status as a "grown up" change things so drastically.

Recently, I spoke at length with a potential client about the changes in his industry. He felt that he needed business owners and personnel with whom he worked to change their principles and beliefs in order for him to be a success in today's market. However, by the end of the discussion, he told me that he wasn't going to make any decisions, spend any money, or take any action until the end of the first quarter because business was so bad. Bear in mind that when I walked through the door of his office, nobody greeted me, and there wasn't a salesperson to be seen. Despite all of his proactive talk, this potential client—and his coworkers—were conditioned to *react*, instead of *act*. Business was not going to magically "get better"; he had to make it better. Waiting for something to happen is for losers. Unfortunately, his reality had become one of scarcity, and in that word, you could hear what was really holding him back—he was scared. As evidenced by his situation, words will only get you so far. It's the belief system behind your words, and the actions that you take because of those belief systems that create any kind of action. Economies don't improve; people improve. And the most important economy is the one created between your ears.

During down markets, you have to get creative to make things happen. Although you can't push a market that's not there, you can find a niche market, create affiliations, utilize your customer base better, and/or push other aspects of your market. In other words, there are alternate options for success, but standing pat and waiting for the world to create your economy is not a good one.

There is an old quote that says, "When you go to work on yourself and get better, it's amazing how much better your customer's get." The one activity that can always pay off during a deteriorating economy is individual and organizational development.

Everything boils down to the four P's of business—People, Process, Product, and Positioning. Do you work daily on your personal development; to increase your knowledge and ability to sell your product; to increase the effectiveness of your process; and to increase your positioning through better marketing? If you do, you will generate your own sales success in good times or bad. Good times will in fact become the norm. Making these efforts on a daily basis requires a clear vision and commitment. Thoreau said it best when he pointed out that, *"Things don't change; people change."* When you dwell on the idea of a bad market, you create the reality of a bad market.

Give the gifts that you have been denying yourself, and decide to become your own personal Santa Claus. Allow no limitations, no excuses, and no reason not to ask and receive. When you open the door to your positive belief system, you close the door of scarcity. When you are suffering from a lack of something, it's because you've allowed yourself to accept this absence. Everything apparent in your outside world of today is a direct reflection of your inside world.

As you improve yourself, you begin to think with a higher level of energy. Think of this as a video game where you have to get a good enough score at one level in order to go to the next level. Once you've improved enough to enter yet another level, you create another opportunity for improvement. The cycle of progress never ends. That's the beauty of sales, business, and life; you never master the game. You always get to improve, and it's this very act of improving that makes it all so much fun.

5

Put Time on Your Side

Action Management vs. Time Management

Everyone wants to succeed. So why is it that all people don't succeed, or reach the level of success that they desire? The answer lies in what I call the **Three Currencies of Success—Money, Talent, and Time.** Everyone spends those three currencies everyday, and learning to maximize the effectiveness of those three currencies can propel anyone to become a sales superstar. In this chapter, we will focus on time. It's the most important of the three currencies because it's the only currency that, once you spend it, you can't get it back.

The three currencies of success must be maximized utilizing the **Four Skills of Success—Sales skills, People skills, Marketing skills, and Life skills.** There are 1,440 minutes in every day, and the difference between success and failure boils down to the actions that you take in that time. "Time management" is a misnomer; the correct term should be

69

"action management." You can't add or delete time, but you can manage what you do with your time. Action management is a *life skill*. Without the right life skills, the other three skills that you need for success—sales skills, people skills, and marketing skills—will not matter.

You have God given talent. You work to educate yourself and hone your skills. Now you must apply the proper actions to turn those skills and talents into moneymakers. Misspent potential talent equals poor results. I have seen many salespeople with great personalities who don't sell squat, because they don't utilize all of that talent wisely with their time.

Salespeople often start out with a focus on the currency of money. However, it's talent and time that actually make you the money. Focusing solely on money not only puts the cart before the horse, but also acts as a repellant against the money you desire. It's common to dwell on the pressures that you place upon yourself to make money. Notice I said that *you* place. The pressures become addictive and cause you to lose sight of how to best use your talent and time to overcome money problems. When you only focus intently on the money and in turn create pressure from those thoughts, you wind up with a **JOB—Just Over Broke**.

Remember that money is nothing more than a paper currency. If you increase your value and use this to increase the value of others, then you can make all the money you desire. Value given = Money received.

A simple definition of a sales superstar is someone who gets much better results than other salespeople. To get better results you must have quantity and quality of actions, or as I always say, "You must quantify to qualify." Let's look at the steps that you must take in order to help maximize your results:

1. Account for your hourly and daily actions.
2. Quantify your good results.
3. Quantify the actions you are taking that lead to those results.
4. Quantify how you can expand your actions.
5. Qualify how you can expand those actions exponentially through others.
6. Quantify how you can automate many of those actions.

7. Quantify your bad results.
8. Quantify the actions that lead to those results.
9. Eliminate or change the actions that don't lead to the results you desire.
10. Create a guard dog approach to your time and the actions you take.

Now let's dig into how the specifics of each one of those steps can lead you to sales superstardom.

1. Account for Your Hourly and Daily Actions

Keep a log for a couple of weeks that details the actions that make up each hour of each day. What do you do when you first get up? Write down the first ten things you do in the morning. Do any of those things contribute to being a sales superstar? Personally, I drink a bottle of water as soon as I wake up. It's a part of my health regimen that I believe contributes to my overall well-being. If I am not healthy, then it's hard for me to sell to the best of my ability. What are the first ten things that you do when you start work? Write them down and analyze them. Do you read the paper, chat with friends, go over the football pool, and go for a smoke? Superstar sales success is created by establishing good habits and patterns. When I started my business, I played a game that I named "Fifty Calls." I tried to make fifty calls each day before I went to lunch. I knew that I might not reach all of my intended customers and may have to leave some messages; but I also knew that if I made fifty calls, I would eventually reach a good number of people.

If you look at my strategy of jumping on the phone and taking action versus making excuses, you can see how the first option would be more likely produce positive results. Over the years I have heard many salespeople make excuses as to why they can't make calls in the morning, or at lunch, or in the late afternoon, or in the evening, or on Saturdays, or even on Fridays. Pretty soon these salespeople have convinced themselves there are only a couple of hours during which they can possibly take action.

Remember that success usually boils down to slight differences in ideas and actions, and that *"small holes cause big flat tires."*

2. Quantify Your Good Results

You must track everything. I am always puzzled at businesses and salespeople who spend tons of money on advertising and marketing, and then don't have any way to measure its results. There is an old adage that says, "50% of advertising does not work, but I don't know which 50%." Your own business does not have to be this way; it is entirely possible nowadays to track your actions and your results. Do you have a call log that you use to determine which ad prompted a call from a customer? Do you use tracking numbers in your marketing? Do you use different numbers or extensions for different ads? Do you know which types of customers, products, or services produce the best margins? If you measure your results, you'll usually find that you can raise asking prices, sell a little less volume, and make a lot more net profit.

3. Quantify the Actions that Lead to Good Results

You then need to take these positive results, and ask yourself questions that will help to determine how to best grow your business. Are you having more success with phone calls, in person visits, or lead generation marketing? Does your selling require that you deal only with decision makers, or do you have a product or service that can be sold through a bottom to top progression? What customers or businesses seem to give you more positive responses? Which customers seem to be easier to reach with fewer gatekeepers? Is there a size of business you do better calling on? Is there a geographic, demographic, or psychographic customer that you get better results from? What methods are getting you good results?

If your calls are working, make more calls. If in-person appointments are bringing you more success, then do less calling and make more face-to-face visits. There isn't a perfect way to sell, but there is a way that works best for *you*. I personally had a lot of success selling by doing in person cold calling, where most people starve to death cold calling. I looked at where they failed and did the opposite. I witnessed the following mistakes (and learned from them):

1. I watched salespeople who went straight to the gatekeeper and who immediately got shut down.
2. I watched salespeople who carried in brochures that ended up in the garbage, and were used like a hall pass for the salesperson to be dismissed.
3. I watched salespeople who did not dress sharply, and failed to maximize their first impression.
4. I watched salespeople try to make presentations standing up without attempting to get the decision maker to sit down.
5. I watched salespeople use language that did not get the customers attention immediately, and neglected to appeal to the decision maker's interests as much as the following might:
   - Making 10% more sales in 3 days
   - Making $10,000 more in 30 days
   - Cutting 10% of expenses in 1 month
   - Reaching 100 more customers in 30 days
   - Getting 10% more repeat customers immediately.
6. I watched salespeople who failed to use words and phrases that showed respect to the decision maker and his time, such as:
   - "I know you are extremely busy"
   - "Very quickly, the reason for my visit . . ."
   - "In 60 seconds I promise to share 3 ways to give you 2 more sales today. If not, then ask me to leave and I will pay you for your time"

What I learned from watching all these other salespeople make mistakes was that success and failure both leave definitive clues. You can dramatically reduce your learning curve to success by not blindly following others. Salespeople often choose to do more of what already has led to their lack of success, simply because that's what they have been told to do.

You must find others who are getting the results that you want and learn how to do what they are doing. Next, keep trying to add more and more avenues to success. More routes will eventually result in more success.

4. Quantify Ways to Expand Your Actions

Now that you know which methods are getting you the results you desire—simply do more of this. I find it strange that when salespeople and businesses discover a successful technique, they often go on to the next tactic before maximizing the thriving process that they have discovered. Its okay to try to develop many successful habits; but don't add more at the expense of spending time perfecting the habits that work.

5. Qualify Ways You Can Expand Those Actions Exponentially Through Others

The next step in the process is to take these successful habits and patterns and multiply their effectiveness. If, for example, phone calls are working for you, then hire and train other people to make additional calls. Average salespeople think too small, and they assume that they can't get others to do what they need, or to do it well enough. Can you get someone to do what you need at 75 percent of your level? If so, then five people operating at 75 percent of your level is much better than going it alone.

Once during a session where I was educating a group of salespeople, one of them mentioned that he had a large catalog of customers. He said that although customers were in a computer database, he had never done anything with the information. I constructed a plan for him so that he would be able to use the database, but when I returned to his office a month later, he hadn't taken any action on it. His excuse was that he did not have the time; my response was that he did not have the time *not* to do it. However, I understood and accepted his objection, and found yet another solution to his problem. I suggested that he hire a high school student to put the plan into action and pay the student to do the work for him. Yet when

I returned another month later, and he still had not gone any further. His excuse this time was that he could not afford to pay someone. My response, once again, was that he couldn't afford not to.

However, I took note of his excuse one more time, and tried to help him find a solution to the problem. I found two other salespeople who were in the same predicament as him; both of these salespeople had neglected their client databases as well, and supposedly had no time to do anything and too small of a budget to pay someone to do it. I put the three together and suggested they hire one person and share the expense, which would make it ridiculously cheap to accomplish what they wanted. I even showed them what to do and how to do it. A month later I checked with the original sales person, and found that he had never taken action on the plan. This time, however, he was out of excuses, and I was out of suggestions for him.

6. *Quantify Ways to Automate Many of Those Actions*

You have more time than you think to create success. Although there may never be a *perfect* time to do something, there can be a right time to do it. There are countless ways to, in essence, buy yourself more time. You can automate repetitive actions with software. You can outsource or delegate tasks—such as the execution of marketing assignments—to others, in order to expand your time in areas that require your concentration. I personally use an online card and postcard program called sendoutcards.com. I can visit their web site and select from thousands of cards to create custom postcards with my own message. I can choose when I want to send them, and design a multi-year campaign in advance, if I desire. This is a perfect example of effective action management through automation.

7. *Quantify the Bad Results You Are Getting*

As a salesperson, you will hear time and time again that selling is a "numbers game." More prospects are supposed to equal more sales. However,

I have often witnessed new salespeople who meet with a mountain of customers without closing any sales. This salesperson is under the impression that the more customers they deal with, the better they will get. This, however, is essentially the definition of insanity: doing more of what you have been doing and expecting different results. You must measure the less-than-stellar results and learn from them. Poor results can help you, but only if you use them to figure out what to do differently. I have a saying: *"stop the train."* If you aren't getting to your destination, then you have to change something.

8. *Quantify the Actions that Lead to those Results and* 9. *Eliminate or Change the Actions That Don't Lead to the Results You Desire*

The example above features a manager who allows his salesperson to practice on her customers. Instead, this salesperson should learn to measure her results and adjust her actions accordingly. This is analogous to the way that flying experts are able to operate a plane. I have taken a few flying lessons from an instructor who is instrument-rated. This means that he can operate the aircraft solely by utilizing his instruments, without visually flying the plane. If you cannot fly a plane to a destination using the instruments, winds and other factors may take your plane off course. But it's your job to constantly monitor your flight pattern and make adjustments to reach your destination safely. Without making these continual adjustments, you are likely to drift off course and fail to land the plane where you had intended. If you measure and monitor the results of your selling actions in the same way, you will be able to adjust just as quickly. Selling, like flying a plane, is a process that requires making constant adjustments.

Patterns of success are rarely perpetual, and what works today might not work tomorrow. The phrase, "If it ain't broke, don't fix it" is a horrible rule to live by. Patterns often become like traditions that you don't want to break. Remember this phrase: "Traditions are made to be a rudder, not an anchor." The superstar salesperson must monitor everything with an almost paranoia-like intensity. Learn to expect the best and plan for the worst. Don't get lazy because you have become drunk with success. Every sale is a new "flight."

10. *Create a Guard Dog Approach to Your Time and the Actions You Take*

Knowing how *not* to spend your time is just as valuable as knowing how to spend it. You must monitor everyone and everything that takes away from your productivity. Once you begin to see how you typically spend your day and what your interruptions are, you can create and implement a plan to guard your most precious currency—your time. Just because you have a phone does not mean you have to answer it. Just because you have email does not mean you have to check it every five minutes. Just because your co-workers want to hang out and chat all the time does not mean you have to join them. You must recognize the factors that rob you of your time, and do whatever you can to eliminate their negative effects.

Exposing Lies of Time Management

There are many things in the world today that are competing for your attention. Multitasking has become a way of life for everyone. Books have even been written about how to master multitasking and be able to handle everything at once. But the truth is that you can't.

Although it seems like everyone has to multitask today to be successful, multitasking is creating a breed of people who spin in circles all day and get little accomplished. When your focus is distracted from the task at hand, you cannot give the attention that is necessary to complete this task or achieve this goal. When you overdo multitasking, you may find that the results of your actions have become less than satisfactory. How often do you find yourself completely forgetting to do certain things, or feeling like you have too much to take care of?

You have to fight the urge to automatically follow the advice that you get from books, CD's, and so-called gurus about multitasking. The devices that are meant help you *manage* your time—such as appointment software or handheld PDAs—might wind up taking more of your time than they could ever save.

In my own experience, this is certainly something that occurs fairly often. I once hired a field sales representative to sell tickets to my seminars. After training the representative, I went with him into the field to observe his progress. After each call he made, he opened up his laptop and entered the contact information into a follow-up software program. This was an example of a good idea with poor execution. My rep was wasting important travel time and possible customer contact time by starting up a laptop, opening a program, and typing information. My own tactic, on the other hand, was to use old-fashioned, 3 × 5 index cards on which I could make notes and attach business cards, and then put in a 3 × 5 file box. Once a week, I gave all the files to someone who could easily enter the information into my follow-up program and hand the files back to me.

My old-fashioned, index card system allowed me to call on twice the amount of clients that my field rep called on in the same amount of time. After only a little while, I managed to sell a tremendous amount more tickets than him. It was hard to convince him to let go of the state of the art technology and his illogical use of it. But since I had been selling my seminars before cell phones became a way of life—okay, so I am dating myself a little here but let me make a point—the method that I had adopted was actually much more productive. I would plan all of my meetings the night before. I would factor in highway traffic patterns, proximities of the businesses, and the amount of time that I was likely to spend at each one. I would then plan to be back in my hotel before the afternoon rush hour had started, so that I could make all my follow-up calls on a stone-age land line telephone.

As cell phones were becoming more prevalent, my early adopter sales reps would laugh at my use of a land line. They felt that the way they did business was more efficient and that they were much more productive because of their cell phones. But I still managed to outsell the people who laughed at me by 3 to 4 times. You might be able to argue that I sold more because I had better sales skills, but what it really came down to was the fact that I used my time more wisely. I took smarter actions that led to better results.

When I rode with my sales reps, I noticed that they would take a lot of calls from friends, spouses, and others that were completely unrelated to business. They were able to make and take these unnecessary calls because they had the technology handy to do it—technology that had become a business interruption device, rather than a productivity tool. I may not have had a cell phone; but I had a better plan, better execution, no interruptions, and much better results. Bottom-line results impress me; gadgets don't.

I don't want to give you the impression that I am strictly an old-school salesperson who is averse to technology and change. I embrace and use technology, and immerse myself in learning it. But more importantly, I figure out how to make the technology work best for me, and expand my productivity. I am extremely wary of using technology in a way that impedes my efficiency. Reading a best-selling book or article on a particular subject doesn't always make the information relevant to you. Just because a new technology comes along, you don't necessarily have to use it. You must use your own judgment to see what works for you.

Time Bandits

You must be as cautious of people as you are of technology. Some people in your life steal your time minute by minute and rob you of income, dollar by dollar. I once had a sales representative that had worked for my company for several years selling tickets to my seminars. The rep had developed a habit of calling me four to six times a day and speaking to me for long periods. He would tell me something at the beginning of the conversation and then he would spend the rest of the time basically repeating or restating. On top of that, he had developed a poor attitude and spent most of the call complaining and discussing the negatives of everything.

The representative had become a tremendous drain on my time and mental health. I tried to explain this to him and counsel him to get better. Meanwhile, his sales numbers were going down the toilet. The rep was offended by my suggestion that he get help. After many efforts to educate the rep to no avail, I had no choice but to fire him. He was shocked and surprised that I had let him go after so many years of working together.

In parting, I tried to explain that his attitude, actions, and habits had become cancerous. I tried to treat the cancer with no success, and now I had to cut the cancer out. Although comparing actions and people to cancer may sound unkind or tough, that's exactly how much I value my time. And I prefer to spend it with, and on, people who are more positive than negative.

You have to take control of exactly what you do with your time, so that you are aware of the type of people and actions on which you spend it. Here are some ways to help control your own *action management*. Try thinking the night before about what you want to accomplish the next day. Think about your larger goals and what your daily tasks will do to contribute to these goals. Write down your goals and your plan each day, and break your day into chunks. To-do lists can often become an enemy to accomplishment. Your goal is to achieve results, not just check off items on to-do lists. In fact, I invite you create a *stop-doing* list. As you did with people who were "time-stealers," figure out which actions in your day are robbing you of your time. What are you doing every day that you should stop doing, or do less of, or delegate to someone else to do? If your current to-do list is made up of actions that are menial and don't create results, then redirect your list, and *"Keep the main thing the main thing"*.

Address all pending actions in your day according to the **Four D's of Action Management—D**o it, **D**ump it, **D**efer it, or **D**elegate it. If an action will make you money, help you or your family grow, or move you towards the accomplishment of a goal, then do it. If the action does not accomplish any those things, then dump it. If the item is something you should do, then decide if you should delegate or outsource it to someone who has more expertise or time to complete the task. *"Don't major in the minor."* If you face a pending action that you must complete yourself but would rather not do right now, write down what the issue or action is and when you must review it in the future. Place the item in a review folder that you will look at every day. When the day for review comes up, look that item over and decide right then to either do it or dump it. Don't defer it any longer. Don't clutter your desk or your mind.

Cell phones, email, fax machines, text messaging, instant messaging, RSS Feeders, and many other technological inventions have created a remarkably "linked" society; but they have brought about unintended consequences as well. They have produced the never disconnected, addicted-to-communication junkie. These technologies generate constant interruptions, which cause you to live by others' schedules instead of your own.

Beware of these time bandits! Sometimes you must disengage from everyone and everything to be able to engage your brain and your actions in a focused and productive way. When you are more productive in your actions you will accomplish more than the distracted masses. The world that we live in today features a society of people who wear their to-do lists on their shirts like a badge of honor. Mr. and Mrs. Busy triumphantly exclaim from the roof tops all that they have to do today for everyone to hear. Unfortunately, though their actions have increased, their results have decreased. The majority of people are working more, working harder, and working for less impressive results.

People, habits, and technology should ideally be tools that we can use to maximize our time. They should help rather than hinder us, and allow us to focus on the best ways to spend our minutes, hours, days, and years. Remember, "Don't major in the minor." Get results with your actions by wisely utilizing your time. *You don't get paid by the hour; you get paid by the value you bring to the hour.*

6

It's All About the Attitude

How to Gain the Attitude of a Sales Superstar

Everyone has probably heard the line, "90 percent of selling is about attitude." That's partly correct, but it's probably more like 99 percent of selling is about attitude. I would even go so far as to claim that 99 percent of *life* is about attitude. It never fails that salespeople with good attitudes outperform salespeople with bad attitudes. Every method discussed in this book is possible to learn and implement with a good attitude. However, this book is not about being good, it's about being great. This book is all about you being a sales superstar. And to become a sales superstar, you must learn to have the superstar's *attitude.*

In my management classes I tell attendees to "hire for talent and attitude, and then train for skills." Given the choice between talent and attitude, I choose attitude every time. Top salespeople are not always the most talented ones in their company; in fact, those who have been labeled as "talented" are the ones who are used to getting by on their natural attributes like looks, personality, or sense of humor. Because of this, these salespeople often do not put as much—or any—effort into improving their skills. They become convinced and enamored with the notion that they are natural-born salespeople who do not need to improve. A "naturally" talented salesperson can learn all of the sales skills and techniques that they want—but unless they use them in conjunction with the proper attitude, they will never get themselves in front of a customer (let alone be an effective salesperson once they do). Meanwhile, salespeople with less talent but better attitudes surpass their results. A superstar attitude applied to action trumps all else.

It's easy to preach to someone about the importance of a good attitude; but how do you really adopt such a frame of mind? When I started selling, every manager I had repeatedly told me to "have a good attitude." Unfortunately, none of them ever told me exactly how to do so. They assumed it was a simple choice—you just say you are going to have a good attitude, and then you do. And I guess that's partially true; but it's not quite that simple.

When I first started selling, I would tell myself over and over that I was going to have a good attitude. Then I would have three customers in a row that I didn't sell to. Next, my managers would yell at me. I would have a disagreement with my girlfriend, and then get caught in the rain and ruin my new shoes. FLUSH! That's the sound of my good attitude going down the toilet. It's easy to say and harder to do unless you have some kind of a system.

Let's develop a plan to cultivate the attitude of a sales superstar. Before you can do that, think about how a typical person's day begins. In fact, let me give you a classic scenario. You wake up, go out into the elements, and get your newspaper. What do you see on the front page? Perhaps a story about how your country is at war, or about the tragedy of Hurricane Katrina. Maybe you see a headline about an earthquake in California, or a devastating tornado in Oklahoma and all the deaths, injuries, and sadness that ensue from such terrible events. Next, you turn to the business section and see that unemployment, inflation, the national debt, credit delinquencies, interest rates, and bankruptcies are all up, and that the stock market and new housing starts are down. As you turn to the stock and mutual fund tables you see that along with all the other news you've received, your personal investments have tanked as well. How is your attitude after reading just two sections?

If you're a glutton for punishment, you turn to the sports section. You see that your favorite football team lost by two touchdowns, the basketball game you bet on cost you one hundred dollars, and your favorite baseball team drafted a kid who, it turns out, is only 15 years old. On top of that, your favorite hockey team hasn't won since Moby Dick was a minnow. Are you pumped up? How's your attitude now?

You go back into your house and turn on the television. Lo and behold the morning news show repeats all the tragedies that you read in the paper. You also learn that there were several murders in your town last night. After you get ready for work, you come downstairs and your kids and spouse hit you up for lunch money. You get into your car (which, to your dismay, your teenager has requested to borrow tonight), and you turn on the radio. The announcer lets you know how badly it snowed last night, that the roads are horrible, and that there are accidents everywhere. You get the feeling that you should really just turn around and go home, and not even attempt the day. Are you feeling better yet?

Let's say, however, that you were brave enough to continue on to work. By the time you get there and pull up, you spot your manager walking in. You can't help thinking about how if you could get him off the phone, you might be able to work some sales deals with him. You also see your finance manager, who is responsible for submitting your customers' applications to lending sources. You contemplate getting him the banks' phone numbers for Christmas; apparently, he has not called them in awhile, since every customer you sell gets turned down for financing. You get out of your car and your response to your colleague's greeting of "good morning" is, "WHY? What's so good about it?" Have you ever lived that day? I certainly have, and if you're being honest, I bet you have too—probably more times than you care to remember.

The question is: What caused you to keep going that day—and what still does? I am a reading junkie, and I love to read newspapers; but if you're the same way, I would suggest that you put off reading them until your selling day is through. You most likely notice that at least 80 percent or more of the news is negative. Newspapers don't tend to print good news, since doom, gloom, and fear are what sell. If you don't believe me, just check out the headlines. Do you realize that the majority of news isn't *really* news; instead, it is planted news. The stories are picked up from news wires, and obviously they are run for a reason. News is, in many ways, marketing and advertising and laden with agendas. Getting all of this information from newspapers, magazines, television, radio, and the Internet essentially bombards your brain with doom, gloom, and fear. It's hard to have a good attitude when you are receiving negative information from multiple news sources on a daily basis.

If you decide that you *must* read the newspaper (as I often do), then try the following: Read the newspaper with an eye toward the fact that much of the content is downbeat and dramatically written; and that no matter what you may read, you cannot allow it to detrimentally affect you and your day. Another way to read the newspaper is to do so from a marketers' perspective, as I try to do. Look at the headlines and ask yourself why writers might have chosen that particular wording. How might you be able use that headline or news story in a headline or marketing effort with your advertising pieces and campaigns? Imagine using the name "Britney Spears" in a headline of one of your promotional pieces, and how doing so could pull readers in to look at your piece. Example: "Britney Spears Tragedy Causes Health Insurance Scare for Many." If you are selling insurance, you might be able to tie the Britney Spears news into the need for disability insurance. You can easily tie current news and events into headlines that will be noticed and increase your sales.

Every day when I read the newspaper, I look for stories and ideas that I can somehow use in my industry. If I read a news, human interest, sports, or business story, I ask how I might be able to apply this to my business or my clients. I am not just looking for headlines, but for portable ideas as well. Often, it only takes a small tweak to create incredible, actionable ideas for immediate use. As I do this, I get incredibly excited and motivated. (Okay, so I am a bit of a marketing geek—but notice that I am taking the usual negative influence of news and making it work for me instead of against me.) By taking this somewhat depressing information and using it for something constructive, you'll bombard your brain with optimism instead. This will definitely have a positive influence on your attitude.

Let's look at a few more ideas that can help you develop a sales superstar's attitude. I am betting that when you get up in the morning, you look in the mirror to shave or put on your makeup. Somewhere on the mirror, I want you to post your top three goals and the sentences that you had written for achieving them. Post your favorite quote, as well as one action that you have to take every day to become a sales superstar—such as creating and sending a postcard follow-up mailing with gifts or an offering to your customers.

Another huge attitude booster is exercise. I personally see a significant positive change in my attitude when I work out regularly. Exercise releases endorphins in your brain that make you feel better and help to increase your confidence. It also allows you to test your endurance and the boundaries of your abilities. People who exercise are more likely to break out of their comfort zones and push their capabilities, while those who don't tend to accept self-imposed limitations and have less endurance. Your mind and your body are undeniably connected, and one greatly influences the other. Exercising one will inevitably make the other stronger.

I personally felt the results of a strong mind-body connection when I developed a strategy to defeat my cancer. It's entirely possible for you to use many of the same techniques that I did to improve your attitude for better sales results. As I mentioned in an earlier chapter, I had a whole regimen that I followed during my cancer treatments. I went through daily radiation treatments: thirty-three in all. Every morning that I had a treatment scheduled, I would arrive at the center long before my appointment time. I would sit in my car and spend time praying and meditating. I wanted to connect my mind and my spirit to improve my overall health.

Next, I did visualization exercises. I would close my eyes and envision Pac Man, from the old video game, on my steering wheel. I would picture Pac Man jumping into my mouth and going to my tonsils where the cancer was, and I would see him gobbling up the cancer. I felt like I could actually hear the chomping. After Pac Man was done eating all of the cancer, he would leap out of my mouth and back onto the steering wheel, and he would spit the cancer out of the window that I had rolled down for him. Pac Man would begin to jump up and down in a strong man pose, and laugh hysterically. I would picture my tonsil healing itself in pink, healthy fashion. I would then play comedy CDs and make a concerted effort to laugh for fifteen minutes or so before I went in for my treatments. Humor and laughter release endorphins that improve mood tremendously; I really do feel that this aided in my healing.

I tried to take a walk or toss a ball with my son every day to stay active. I drank tons of water, and ate natural, healthy foods to bolster my immune system. I visited a doctor who advised me on the best ways to detoxify my whole body and increase the strength of my immune system. I went to bed early at night, and made sure that I got lots of sleep and rest. I read various books and online reports about my disease to educate myself. Why do I share all this with you? Because it shows you that I had a game plan. I was empowered and in charge. I kept myself busy with healing and wellness, and all of these things helped me to maintain a fantastic attitude.

This experience showed me how important "mind over matter" really is—in both my career and my personal life. It's easy to blame a bad economy for poor sales, but as I've mentioned before, the only economy that really matters is the one you create in your head. People spend a lot of time worrying about, for example, who the next President is going to be. They wonder how this is going to affect their lives. Yet they don't spend nearly enough time considering how their own attitude affects their lives. The truth is that your outlook and mindset will affect your life more than any President who has been or ever will be elected. Start with your own personal world; then you can worry about the rest.

How to Maintain a Sales Superstar Attitude

This flow chart is a tool that can you help to maintain a superstar attitude. Write it out and put this at your desk, in your car, or wherever you operate your sales empire from.

1. Thoughts
2. Emotions

3. Words
4. Actions
5. Habits
6. Results
7. Character
8. Destiny

Your attitude is based upon your thoughts. In Napoleon Hill's *Think and Grow Rich* (BN Publishing, 2007), the author talks about how your thoughts create your reality. What thoughts do you have everyday? Which ones seem to recur the most often? The thoughts you have today create your reality tomorrow. You are in charge, so choose your thoughts wisely. Take the top five things you want to dwell on and tape them to your steering wheel, your desk, and your mirror. Consider the emotions that these thoughts evoke. What do you think and how do you feel when you are taking successful actions? Picture a potential sale that you will make that day, and anchor those thoughts and feelings in. Consider the habits that you are forming, one of which should be rewriting your goals every morning. Make yourself dwell habitually on your positive attitude, and on the attitude you have when you get the results you like.

My son Jake's Pee Wee football coach sent an email out to the parents of the team members at the beginning of the season. The email acknowledged that going through the dog day practices in 100 degree heat in July and August was not fun. Having sweat dripping in your eye and burning is not fun. Getting hit and knocked on your butt is not fun. Learning how to play the game, to trust and enjoy your teammates, to get more from yourself than expected, to get better everyday, and winning—these, however, are all fun. Some of the parents had a hard time with that concept, since it's difficult for parents to accept that their young children are not always going to have fun. For some parents, the reality of the email seemed a bit too harsh.

Jake's football team became the first team from our town to win the Super Bowl in their league for any age group. The team played extremely well and at an advanced level for their age. Many people said they were the most disciplined team at any age level in a league of many teams. This was a feat accomplished completely by seven and eight-year-olds. Their coach was right. He created an atmosphere and habit of a superstar attitude. The Super Bowl was just the physical manifestation of the team's attitude; it had already been won from the very first practice. Yes, I can assure you that the kids had a ton of fun. However, you should have seen their attitude transfer to the parents—it was contagious. Even those who had originally had a problem with the coach's concepts were inspired. Superstar attitudes have a tendency to spread.

When I was selling my seminars—when I went on a sales call, or was going to do a sales meeting—I would yell "Showtime!" moments before. Yelling "Showtime" reminded me that this was my "Showtime," and I had to be ready to perform. The customers did not care if I had an argument with my wife. They did not care if my bills needed to be paid. They did not care that I had just dealt with an unhappy employee or client. The customers care about themselves, and what I can do for them. I owe them "Showtime." Just yelling the word gets your blood pressure up, and moves you out of your comfort zone, in the same way that athletes get pumped up before a game, musicians warm up before a performance, and actors say their lines before the curtain goes up. Salespeople must do the same.

You might be saying, "That sounds great—but I deal with some real jerks, and I face a lot of rejection." To be a sales superstar, you must accept rejection as part of the game. Regular salespeople get so deflated by rejection that they wear it on their sleeve and they carry it into the next sales attempt. You can learn from what went wrong with this situation, but you cannot let it take control of your attitude.

During my time managing the auto dealership, I saw many salespeople experience a week of no sales, followed by a visible slump. I would see them walk out to greet a customer with their shoulders all hunched over and speaking in a monotone voice. All the energy they emanated was laden with failure. It was almost as if they were saying "Hi, I know you don't want to buy anything, and I probably couldn't help you if you did, so let's get this out of the way. However, my kids are starving and I am going to lose my job, so if you feel pity on me then please, please buy a vehicle." You can imagine how the average customer might react to such an introduction!

Remember this: *You are the same person after the sales attempt as you were before.* Nothing has changed because you attempted to make a sale. You simply had an unsuccessful attempt. *Never get too high, and never get too low.* I have seen salespeople get so pumped up after a sale and are so busy patting themselves on the back that they miss five new opportunities, because they are not prepared to use the positive momentum. I have also seen many times where salespeople fail and begin to internalize the result as a personal affront. Somehow, in their minds, a failed sales attempt makes them failures as people.

You must view the missed sale as part of the whole picture, rather than just as one event. By doing so, you can turn the negative into a positive. If a good closing ratio in your industry is 33 percent, then just look at a missed sales attempt as a step that was necessary to take in order to end up with a positive result. Although I don't like the phrase, "It's a numbers game" in reference to sales, because I think it trivializes the customer, there is some truth to the fact that you will encounter more lost than won sales on your path to sales superstardom. Look at the missed sales—even the ones where you have to deal with the occasional jerk—as a positive. If you let a negative person affect you mentally for just one minute—let alone a whole day or week—you will allow this person to control your destiny and doom your results. Never give anyone that much power over you and your success (especially a jerk!).

The next time you deal with someone like this, simply do the very best you can and kill him with kindness. Sometimes, he'll wind up being a nice person who is simply afraid to make a mistake or be taken advantage of, and is disguising his fear with a nasty demeanor. Either way, once you're finished dealing with the jerk customer, thank them repeatedly. Chances are he will be puzzled as to why you are being so kind to him. Since you are going to be saying to yourself that you know that 1 out of 20 people you deal with is like this, then your chances are looking pretty good the rest of the week! You determine your attitude; don't let him do it.

After every sales attempt, I would invite you to use what is probably the most important word in sales—NEXT! Whether you make a sell or you don't, I encourage you to yell NEXT! Don't worry who hears you, or whether they think you are crazy or not. You must energize your attitude and get yourself ready to move immediately to the next step. You must not muddle around in a haze over a missed sale, or sit back and relax while you count the commission on the sale you just made. Just say NEXT! If you do make a sale, you should immediately use that as momentum and an attitude-builder to propel you into action for the next sale. Make sure to recognize and use the things that worked best in that sale to create successful sales habits.

How to Protect Your Income from the Brain Snatchers

It's a fact that success breeds jealousy, envy, and enemies. Some people will always have something negative or limiting to say about you and your success. Sales superstars develop incredibly thick skin, and while they may not be immune to criticism, they come damn close.

When you become a sales superstar, some salespeople might say that you cherry-pick the good customers, or that it's beginners luck, or that you are the boss' pet or "house mouse," and that you get fed all the house deals. You have to simply laugh and move on. Giving one minute of anger to their insecurities is a minute wasted.

There is a saying, "Be wary of advice and counsel." Take this saying to heart. The person with the advice is often the same person who couldn't sell food to a starving crowd and someone who will attempt to inhibit your success in many ways—such as coming to your desk when you are busy making outbound calls. My friend, the late Bill West, used to do one of two things to counteract this interference. As soon as someone would attempt to sit down he would say he was sorry, but he had to make a private call—and he would pick up the phone and start dialing. Or, he would stand up and say he had to run a quick errand. As soon as the person left, he returned and got busy. I watched Bill make hundreds of contacts each day, intelligently using his database of customers and "bird dogs." He simply worked wisely so that he did not have to work particularly hard or for nearly as many hours as other salespeople did. Yet he made a lot more sales, and a lot more money. Bill was the perfect example of a sales superstar that would not let the brain snatchers take his time or his positive attitude.

In order to keep your day focused on positive energy, make sure to take note of who the negative salespeople and even managers are in your organization. Sometimes, it is the managers who will try the hardest to bring you down. Don't let them. Realize that their attempts are just borne of jealousy. Make sure that your day is packed tightly with activity. Action creates action. When you are busy, it is hard to be pessimistic. Negative people will tend to move more toward other negative people, because they are more comfortable with them. Negative people don't want to sit in the shadow of your sunshine.

Make a list of at least three things that you can do each hour to make yourself feel satisfaction, reward, and achievement. All of these things will enhance a positive attitude. Don't wait for them to happen—plan them. Nature abhors a vacuum. If you leave too much empty time with no positive plan for that time, you can bet that the evil and negative brain snatchers will appear.

I also believe that you have to plan rest, recreation, and sabbaticals for physical and mental health in order to maintain a superstar attitude. People often don't want to talk about the need to recharge your batteries and how necessary that is for you to remain successful—in sales and in life. Sales people who run on low batteries don't perform as well as when they are charged up. A while back, I went on a cruise with my family, and had a fantastic trip. We went scuba diving in Grand Turks, and during the dive, had three dolphins come up and play with us for most of the dive. The dive masters on the trip told us that it was a once in a lifetime experience—not only to see the dolphins, but to have them play with us for so long. What if we had decided not to take the trip? What if our fears had kept us from becoming certified divers years ago? I have never left a vacation saying I should take fewer vacations; I have, however, forgone vacations because of business or other concerns. I realize now that this is shortsighted thinking. Vacations allow you to experience great things, and give you a chance to recharge your batteries. Time off from your daily activities—especially time spent in a different place—can provide a much-needed different perspective.

Have you ever skipped taking time off because of a lack of money or time? Consider the mindset that allows you to initially believe that you don't have enough time or money to take a vacation. To replace this outlook, you must first take the time to evaluate the thoughts that led to your reluctance to give yourself time off. You must begin to change those thoughts and actions. I think that we often tend to get caught up in our day-to-day actions and problems, and we lose our best perspective. Proper rest is one of the key ingredients to good health. This includes rest for the mind, as well as the body. A few years ago, I made the choice to get one more hour of sleep a night. The difference that this made in my vitality of mind and body was remarkable. Awaking with a clear mind and body can improve your appearance and a customer's first impression of you. When you recharge your batteries, you allow your mind to give and receive answers that it cannot when you are tired.

Our culture often promotes the maxim of hard work. However, I don't think it is necessary to associate work with being "hard." The connection that forms in your mind about work being hard and being a grind can be counterproductive. Most salespeople will attest to the fact that there are times when they are on a roll, and in the flow, and everything they touch turns to gold. I don't believe those times are accidental. I believe those periods of seemingly easily attained success are attributable to previous thoughts and actions. Those successful thoughts and actions are easier to achieve when you are rested and clear of anything interfering with your mind or body.

Because our culture lends a great amount of macho bravado to the custom of hard work, the notion of resting, thinking, and recharging your batteries is considered weak by many. In the past several years, I have found that one's quality of work is more important than endurance and ability to "work hard." Negative thoughts and actions done over a longer period of time can never be as productive as positive thoughts and actions exhibited during a short period of time.

Parkinson's Law is a theory that states that work fills up to the time allotted. The more time you allow, the more you find to do. The question is, what are you really doing? I would encourage you today to analyze your actions, the people you are with, and how they add to or subtract from your superstar attitude. Think of yourself as a bank. With each action you take or each person you encounter, you are you making a deposit or withdrawal in the account of your sales superstar attitude.

See If Your Wheel Will Roll

Look at each area in the diagram. Each circle represents an important part of your well being. Grade yourself from 1–10 (10 being perfect) on your current satisfaction in each area. If you were a 10 in every area, your life

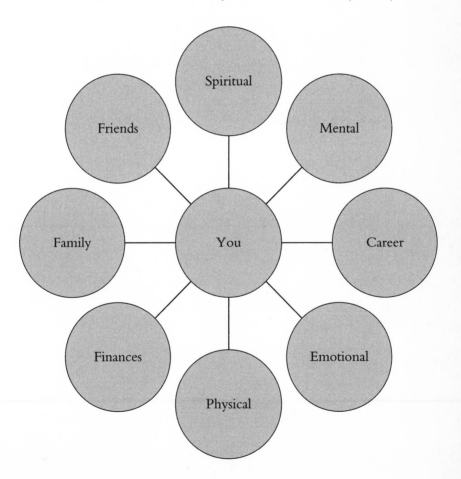

would be like a wheel that turns easily. However, there are always areas that you need to work on. Be careful not to spend all of your time on one weak area, because when you concentrate on only one area, you tend to disregard the others. You therefore may continually be trying to fix flat tires. Instead, try to work on each area a little bit every day, and constantly tone each area up. Obviously, nobody is perfect, and you are always a work in process. Each area is connected to the other, and each area affects your attitude. And we know—it's all about attitude!

7

Lead Generation = $ Creation

Why Over 90 percent of Salespeople Underachieve

As a salesperson, you must view what you do as a *business,* instead of simply a job. You must take total ownership for both the good and bad results that you produce. If you are employed by a company, look at your paycheck each pay period, and know that you are responsible for the amount that's there. The company merely gives you a check; you fill in the numbers. If you run your own business, your accountant prints out a financial statement; but again, you fill in the numbers. Whatever your official status is, you need to realize that a business or a career rises or falls based on two areas of competency—people skills and marketing skills. You have to become an expert at marketing, and produce a steady stream of customers to become a sales superstar.

Sales people who have great sales and people skills but who are poor marketers will struggle in today's economy. In 1950, the average person was probably exposed to about 100 marketing messages a day, and of these 100 messages, maybe ten would ask the customer to buy something or do something now. By 1980, this number had risen to an exposure of 1,000 messages daily, with 100 of those asking the person to buy or take action. Fast forward to today and those numbers are probably more like 10,000 messages a day with 1,000 being action-oriented. The bottom line is that there is a tremendous amount of competition for the attention of your potential customers. You have to be able to cut through the clutter and generate leads. **Lead generation = Dollar creation.**

Many people get into sales and think that their employers will provide the prospects; or, if they own a business, think that all they have to do is hang out a sign for people to start knocking their door down. I'm sorry to be the bearer of bad news for folks who believe the flood gates of profit will automatically open; but chances are that these people are doomed. For instance, while many franchisors offer a lot of training on how to operate a specific product, service, or store, few offer any real training on marketing the *business.* If you were to look at the franchisees who fail, you'd notice that it's likely due to the fact that they didn't know how to get customers interested initially.

You have to work as hard or harder *on* the business as you do *in* the business. Working on the business means concentrating on items like the creation of lead-generation machines. Wouldn't it be nice to have a steady stream of clients who have expressed interest in what you have to sell, rather than wondering where your next prospect and customer will come from? Wouldn't it be nice if you had interested customers contacting you instead of having to cold call for patrons? Smart marketing makes this happen.

Over 90 percent of salespeople remain in what I call "Roller Coaster Hell" for the majority of their sales careers. One month is good and they have a good number of customers, but the next month leaves them high and dry. One month, they are working leads, and following up; then at the end of the month, those deals close, and they're left with nothing. The problem is that all of their effort has been concentrated on working those existing customers—and now the pipeline is empty. The customer flow and work flow is uneven; feast or famine is the norm. These slow periods cause panic, and when salespeople panic, they either quit or look for greener pastures. They search for a business that provides more leads or more advertising so that they can obtain more customers. But the greener pastures often don't appear as green when they arrive there; in fact, they dry up and turn brown very fast. This is why, to be a superstar salesperson, you must think long-term as well as short-term. You have to find a way to keep the grass green, and keep the customers coming.

Most salespeople think of marketing as advertising, and never feel that they have enough money or resources to advertise. Fear of a cash crunch can keep a salesperson from building a sustainable business. This is a mistake, and a perfect example of what I have previously referred to as the *"When-Then Syndrome."* This salesperson waits until he makes more sales to begin a marketing push. However, it is entirely possible to market effectively with a small budget; I will share several low to even no-cost marketing techniques that can elicit potential customers. Secondly, if you knew that you could spend $1 and get back $2 in return—how many dollars would you spend? How many ways could you find to obtain the money that you would need to do that? There is never a lack of money; you may simply lack education on how to earn this money. Once you figure out how to spend money on resources that provide a profit and return on investment, you will begin to find ways to fund your marketing budget.

I once heard marketing guru Dan Kennedy say something that I thought was brilliant: "Most people look for one way to get one hundred customers; but you should really look for one hundred ways to get one customer." Marketing is a never-ending journey of discovering multiple ways to get and keep customers, profits, and return on investment. But far too often, salespeople are their own worst enemies. Here is a common scenario: A salesperson takes a leap of faith and tries to implement some form of marketing. Maybe he gets the idea that an ad in a newspaper or a magazine is the way to acquire business. Or maybe he decides to send sales letters, hoping people will respond; or maybe he makes a hundred cold calls. But none of his efforts bring forth any results. The salesperson declares that the marketing process he chose does not work for his industry, and that his attempts were a waste of money.

When marketing doesn't produce positive results, fear, shock, and anger loom large in the mind of the salesperson; and those feelings prevent the salesperson from trying again. He believes that he tried the process, and the results are proof that the process does not work. The salesperson is both right and wrong; he is wrong in his thoughts and approaches, but right in his theory that this particular approach did not work. Still, he does not understand that it is okay to fail, and that failure doesn't last forever. No matter how good a marketer you are, you will likely fail more times than you win. The key is to make your wins pay handsomely enough that they cover your losses, and then some. Marketing is never a straight line; it is never a black and white, right or wrong proposition. Good marketing takes an incredible amount of trial and error, and testing and measuring. Fortunately, you can learn from the successes and failures of your peers, and can even gather enough information from watching others to avoid some of your own failures. This takes sustained effort. If you begin to execute a strategy of marketing and don't immediately enjoy success, you can't quit—even though it's easier to say something doesn't work than it is figure out how to turn this failure into triumph. As a small marketer in the Internet age, you can give the impression that you are bigger and more successful than you really are. You can create a thriving brand. You can be more agile and target more accurately than larger businesses that have much bigger budgets. Even overhyped, overcompetitive marketplaces are perfect for today's dedicated and creative salesperson.

Let's discuss what you can do to maximize your success.

Marketing, Marketing, Marketing!

Your first step is to create a marketing web. Here is a three-step strategy to create the web.

1. Draw a small circle in the middle of a piece of paper in which you write the initials of your business. Remember that this is *your* business, so name it whatever you want.

2. Draw lines that extend out from the circle. Write down a source for leads and customers on each line. The first two options that you list might be, for example, walk-ins or phone prospects—both of which are produced by your business or employer and are therefore sources over

which you have no control. You must be in command of your own destiny, and think of ways to produce customers from other resources. What other sources of leads did you list? Some suggestions are: referrals, service department, service tickets, be-backs (or unsold customers), affiliations (other industries, vendors), repeat buyers, targeted phone calling, database marketing (current or past customers), targeted list mailings (list vendors, magazine subscribers, SRDS Guide), orphan customers (customer base whose salesperson is no longer employed by your company), lost customer marketing (your inactive customers who have not done business with you in a while, or are now buying elsewhere), coupon swaps, joint venture advertising (other businesses or vendors), community boards (YMCA, grocery stores, apartment buildings, and Internet community or discussion boards), flyers (distributed in parking lots or businesses), door-to-door flyers, web sites, email marketing (opt-in lists of your own or other vendors and affiliates, third party opt-in lists for rent), social networks (MySpace, FaceBook, Digg), blogging (MySpace, WordPress, Blogger), bird dog programs (paying current customers and others to bring you customers and rewarding them), and many more. Never stop adding strands to your web.

3. For each source, choose at least one strategy of creating leads. If you execute one strategy a day on ten ways to create leads, your leads will grow exponentially over time. Your business will hit a period of critical mass and explode. At the critical mass point, a sales person has the best job in his company. Your pay, hours, stress level, and job security are better than that of the managers. Your risk is less, your investment minimal, and most everything is supplied for you.

Why don't more salespeople take this road to success? Usually, they hesitate because they lack personal buy-in. If you haven't begun to create a business of your own, then your belief system doesn't buy into the idea of a self-created destiny in sales. Either you have "Manageritis" and think the security and prestige of being a manager is the way to go; or you don't believe that selling is a career for you; or you don't believe you will be at your current employer in the future, so why bother; or you don't believe it can be done; or you're lazy. The truth can be hard to face sometimes, and the truth is that success and failure are all about belief systems and habits.

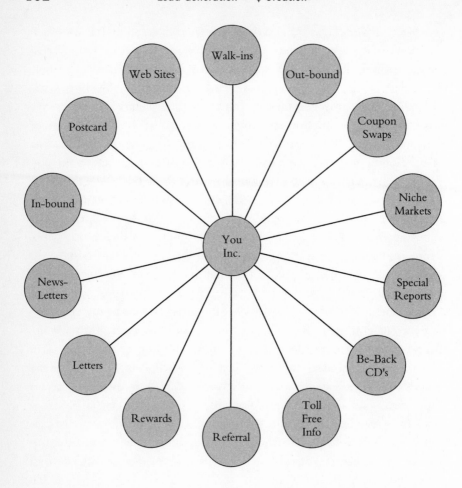

Now let's talk about how to build a strong marketing web and make it last.

Five Ways to Increase the Bottom Line of Any Business
1. Sell more.
2. Increase profit margins.
3. Increase repeats.
4. Increase speed or cycle of repeats.
5. Create a continuity program.

When you are creating a marketing program, you should address each one of these opportunities for growth in as many ways as possible. Most people just look to option 1, to sell more of whatever it is that they sell, and maybe design an ad to push the product or service. Advertising is often a one-step process: you advertise and ask someone to buy, and they either do or don't. Unfortunately, the costs are usually high and do not allow much margin for error for a salesperson.

Instead of one-step marketing, which simply asks someone to buy, I want you to start thinking in multistep lead generation programs. For example, you might run a small ad (called a liner ad) in the back of a trade journal that offers a FREE Special Report with ten tips to solve your customer's biggest headache or problem, and you provide a toll-free number to order. Or, you can provide this number to compel someone to call, have him listen to a recorded message, and then tell him at the end of the message how to leave his information to get the report. Or, you could direct a potential customer to a landing page on a web site that asks him for his contact information; and when he submits the information, the site uses an email auto responder to automatically send him the report. You can direct people to your blog for the information. Doing these things asks the customer to raise his hand to show interest. You aren't asking customers to buy; instead, you are asking them to show you that they want to know more. It's much easier for a customer to request information than it is for him to take action to buy. You must become a source of education for your customers. Creating multiple step lead generation programs will benefit you in many ways. The first is that this mode of marketing is usually much cheaper than traditional advertising—such as displaying ads in newspapers or magazines. Secondly, this type of promotion usually produces qualified customers who have gone through two or more steps in the process, and have acknowledged both their pain and their desire to find a solution, or their interest in what you have to offer.

By using the marketing web strategy I described above, you are creating a business that does not depend on just one source for leads. The more sources, strategies, and techniques that you employ, the less chance you have for failure. Think of your marketing strategy as a building that is bolstered by multiple support columns versus just one. When one source is not producing as well, chances are that at least one other will be. You must think in terms of multiple streams of lead generation. This was once described to me as a *river of nickels*. You create a river of nickels that flow into an ocean of dollars.

When you create your marketing strategies, you must always take the time to review a few items:

1. **TLC (Think Like a Customer)** – Am I thinking like a customer when I am developing this? The legendary copywriter and marketer Claude Hopkins said "you must enter into the conversation already going on in the customer's head." Their need for whatever you are providing existed before you let them know that you could provide it. You must try to approach the situation from their point of view and write or talk to them in what is known as the *buyer's language*.

2. **WIIFM (What's In It For Me?)** – The customer wants you to say specifically what you have, and exactly how this will benefit him or her. Customers want to know how you can resolve their pain, their fears, or their problems; or how you can give them something they want.

3. **SDP (Specific Defining Proposition)** – The customer wants you to identify precisely why you are unique, or why you and your product or service is the best choice. You must answer these four questions specifically.

1. Why is your product or service the best choice?
2. Why is your business the best choice to deliver it?
3. Why are you the best salesperson to deliver what's promised?
4. Can you be trusted?

If you are able to answer these questions definitively, you are in a much better position to provide specific and relevant information to your potential customers.

4. **Leverage** – Ask yourself: Does your marketing strategy or technique provide enough leverage to make someone want to respond? Do you provide a compelling story? Remember, *"Facts tell, stories sell."* In other words, it is good to have customers who can speak of their own positive experiences with you. Do you have strong and specific testimonials?

"If someone else toots your horn, it will be heard twice as far and twice as long." Use customer anecdotes that cite specific results and that can directly name and quote the person who received these remarkable results. However, you don't want to use testimonials that say you were a great salesperson. People don't care about your ability; they care about what they get. Do you offer strong guarantees, that can, if possible, be unconditional? Another way to think of this is to ask yourself: Do you offer **Risk Aversion and Risk Reversal?** In other words—do you reduce or eliminate all risk for the customer upfront, and then demonstrate how you will guarantee that? For example, offering a free special report is a risk aversion technique. Offer to pay someone if you can't deliver what you promise is risk reversal. My best advice is to create leverage by using risk aversion and reversal strategies that are stronger than ten fields of garlic. An example of this is the guarantee I offer attendees to my sales management workshops.

The Tewart Five Way Better Than Money Back Guarantee

1. You receive an unconditional guarantee.
2. You can even take up to thirty days after the program to decide.
3. You can keep all the educational materials even if you want your money back ($2,500 value).
4. I will reimburse you up to $500 in travel expenses.
5. I will refund double your enrollment fee.

In all of my years offering this guarantee, I have never had anyone ask for their money back. I knew that my course was good enough, and that I would not be taking much risk by making the offer. But at the same time, I knew that doing so would eliminate my customer's risk. You must make your guarantee as strong as possible.

5. **Call to Action** – When you are executing a marketing strategy, you must be clear on what you want the customer to do. If there is any confusion on the customer's part as to what is expected of them, then you lose. Do you want the customer to call a certain number to receive a particular offer? Do you want a customer to respond by a specific date? Do you want the customer to go to a website and submit their contact information to

receive a gift or special offer? Be clear about what steps the customers must take, and don't be shy in asking them to do so.

6. **Use Scarcity** – Value tends to go up in proportion to the scarcity of an item or idea. If you believe that you have "The Secret;" or your report can only be offered to the first nineteen people to respond; or if you have only nine slots for your service; then you will create scarcity. When you provide unlimited access or goods in any way, you lessen your value. PLEASE REMEMBER THIS: *Scarcity motivates people to action.* Every holiday season, there is a rush of people shopping for the elusive hot toy or gift of the year. They always want the gift that they feel might not be available because of a limited supply. People desire what they can't have or might not be able to get. Customers don't want to be left out, and they don't want to feel like others were able to get ahead of them.

7. **Value vs. Price Proposition** – All customers form instant opinions of an item's value versus its price. Having the lowest-priced product or service is not always the best idea, since too low of a price can lessen an item's perceived value. Having a high price, but adding significance through extras and add-ons, can create value. Have you ever seen something for a really low price, and wondered what was wrong with it? Have you ever seen something that was a higher priced than what you had expected, and wondered what made it so much better? There really is no "correct" price, but the real question to ask is: what is the correct *value*? You can constantly test your product or service with attached goods or services to add worth to it. You can also bundle your product or service with other items to provide a package. Often, the more items in a package or the more bonuses you add, the higher the perceived value of the item. For instance, you can offer ten bonus items when your customer buys the original product. These items don't have to cost you much money, but they can provide a lot of value. Remember that information is usually free, is always valuable, and can be used as a resource. For example, our materials for many of the industries for which we provide customized education include online education modules, an educational DVD, and other productivity tools. These items are included in the fee and shown as bonuses. Always try to add value that goes above and beyond your core offering with bonuses and freebies. It increases the value of the offer, takes focus off

of the price consideration of your product or service, and elevates you in comparison shopping with your competitors.

8. **Law of Reciprocity** – If someone gives you an item or provides something of great value to you, you begin to feel obligated to give back. You feel like you should reciprocate the value. This reciprocation of value and obligation to give back is crucial in marketing and selling. You must try to provide as much as possible in the way of information, education, methods to avoid rip-offs and fraud, ways to save money and time, and other resources. For example, an automotive salesperson should create a free special report titled "Ten Things You Should Know Before You Buy a Vehicle," or "The Seven Deadly Mistakes You Can Make When You Buy a Vehicle." Again, this is an item that costs the salesperson next to nothing, but that provides a great amount of value for his customer.

The Reverse Funnel Theory

Earlier in the chapter, I mentioned that salespeople can easily get caught up in "Roller Coaster Sales Hell," which is what occurs when you work hard in the business—but don't have a way to simultaneously work *on* the business in order to generate more leads. Instead of establishing a pattern like this, you must attempt to create a reverse funnel. This will provide a constant flow of customers, and will keep you from starving at the beginning of each month because you are out of customers. It will allow you to work both *in* and *on* the business.

To create a "Reverse Funnel," you must consistently ask yourself an important marketing question: "Who does business with the people I want to do business with?" Specifically:

1. Are there companies in non-competitive fields that are successfully doing business with the customers you would like to have?
2. Are there organizations or associations that have membership rolls that are comprised of the customers you would like to have?
3. Are there suppliers or vendors that provide services or material for the companies with whom you want to do business?

4. Are there trade magazines or newsletters that interact with or reach the customers with whom you want to do business?

You've already identified who your potential resources are. Now you must try to create alliances with them. Determine if there is a company selling a non-competitive product that has been conducting business in an enduring and endearing manner with the customers whom you desire to have. Your first step would be to contact a key employee in the company and propose a value proposition to reward them (and in return, reward yourself as well). For example, you might offer to send a letter to every customer in your database introducing their company, and that will provide a strong inducement for them to do business with this new firm. You will do the work and bear the expense, and they will reap the rewards. Of course, you would suggest that the same offer apply to you, in regards to providing an introduction to their customers.

Believe it or not, such a proposal really can work quite well; and in my own experience, I've found that it *does* work quite well. I once went with an automotive salesperson to a local, family-owned restaurant that had great food and a strong community following. We introduced ourselves to the owner, and I told him that if he would allow me ten minutes or less, I could show him a way that I could significantly increase his business on the worst day of the week for him—and I could do it for free. All I asked was for him to sit down for the ten minutes of his time that it would take. I told him if he got the impression that I wasn't capable of doing what I had promised after the ten minutes, that he could ask me to leave. The owner agreed, and we sat down.

I asked him what his slowest day of the week was, and he told me that it was Monday. I told him that my companion was a representative from a local automobile dealership that hundreds of customers visited every day. They came in for the sales, finance, service, parts, and body shop departments. I told him that this dealership representative would create a coupon, at his own expense, that would create a lot of business for the restaurant on Mondays—perhaps an offer for a two-for-one special on Mondays only. I let the owner know that the dealership, and specifically, this representative, would pass out these coupons to the receptionist, the cashier, the sales floor, the finance department, and the service, parts, and body shop departments. I told him we would enclose the coupons in notices, newsletters, and billings from the dealership, and that the coupon would reward our customers with a valuable two-for-one special for a good meal at his restaurant. In return, it would build his business on a weaker day, allow him to acquire new customers, and have old ones return. His restaurant would turn new customers into habitual customers, and keep his already loyal customers in the fold. All he had to do was make the offer. If they upsold a dessert or a drink, or if the coupon holders brought other people with them, then they would instantly profit from the coupon—and also from the value of a long-term customer.

The restaurant owner was pleased with the idea and immediately agreed. He then asked what he could do for us. I told him that the dealership representative would like to create a coupon from the dealership that the owner could use to reward his customers. Every time a waitress laid down a check, she would include one of the dealership coupons, which would state that the coupon was only redeemable with *this* dealership representative. The owner agreed to this part of the proposal as well, and once the plan was set into motion, everyone involved enjoyed fantastic results. The restaurant experienced a steady stream of customers on what had been their worst day of the week, and the salesperson began to get leads to sales and customers.

Such a win-win strategy is hard for any business owner to pass up, but you have to make sure that you think in terms of rewarding the business owner first. You are utilizing the relationships the business owner has with his customers for some sweat equity and an offer that you can make. Think of the unlimited supply of businesses you could work with using this technique. Even if you're a brand new salesperson with a database of zero existing personal customers, this would allow you to instantly create leads, relationships, and customers.

Don't Give up so Easily . . .

Salespeople are always looking for new leads; but they often don't expend enough effort to maximize the leads that they already have. Studies have often shown that salespeople never follow up with most unsold customers. Those customers eventually do buy, and if you don't follow up, they have to buy from someone else. Wouldn't it better if it were from you?

Most salespeople could significantly increase their closing ratios, sales numbers, and incomes if they could simply learn how to transfer more of their unsold customers. Let's look at some ways to convert unsold customers—which are often referred to in sales as *Be-Backs*. The following can help transform more of your Be-Back leads into sold customers.

Create a Be-Back CD

When customers have decided not to buy, you should give them what I call a Be-Back CD. Try the following:

1. You will have recorded a CD to give to customers who've decided against buying. Ask them to play this CD on the way home, or offer send it to them in the mail and ask that they play it when they receive it.

2. When you record the CD, start off by thanking your potential customer for the chance to do business with them, and for taking just a couple of minutes to listen in their car or at home.

3. Tell the customers to make sure to listen all the way to the end of the CD to learn how they can get their free gift.

4. Explain your SDP (Specific Defining Proposition) – Discuss exactly what makes you, your business, and your product or service the best for the customer. Tell your story, and tell it well; but most importantly, relate it to the customer's interests.

5. Include some testimonials that you can either record directly from your current customers, or that you can read (or have someone else read) that quote the customers.

6. Create a bonus offer or incentive to reward your potential customers.

7. Give a free gift to make them come back to you, or have them set up another appointment to get the free gift. There's no harm in bribing them shamelessly.

8. Restate your contact information. Give phone numbers, toll-free numbers, email addresses, and direct them to your personal web site for your free special reports. Overwhelm the customer with evidence that it's a pleasure to do business with you.

Sell the Neighbors

If you sell a product or service to the public, go to the library every time you make a sale and use the City Directory (also known as the Crisscross Directory) to get names and addresses of the customer's closest neighbors. You can send a postcard telling them that you just sold a widget to their neighbors at 1111 Main St., make an offer to them, and also offer a gift for taking action.

Sell the Neighbors, Friends, and Relatives

When customers buy from you, they probably like and trust you. Use the strength of your bond with customers to ask them for referrals—however, you must learn to do this correctly. When I first started selling, I didn't know how to ask for referrals in the right way, and therefore, I never received any. But once I changed the manner in which I asked—my referrals shot up. Here's an example of how a follow-up conversation with a customer might go:

1. "Hi, this is Mark Tewart with ABC Company. How are you today? Am I reaching you at a good time?"
2. "Great! The reason for my call is I am following up after your purchase to make sure everything is good."
3. "Do you have any questions?"
4. "Did you receive my thank you card, and my gift?"
5. "John, when you bought from me, two things happened. One is I gained a customer and the second is I lost my best prospect. Because I live by prospects, I need your help."

6. "John, I wanted to ask you a question. Out of all of your friends, relatives, neighbors, and co-workers, who would you say would be the *most* likely to buy a widget in the next six months?"

Ask for referrals from the people to whom you sell, and also from the ones to whom you don't. People will often refer you to others, even if you couldn't be the one to sell to them.

Use the SRDS—Standard Rate and Data Service

If you go the library, you will find this guide in the reference section. Study it in detail; it will help you to come up with tons of niche marketing ideas. Let's say that you sell products that are geared towards horse owners. Find the horse trade or interest magazines and get in touch with them. See if the magazines' lists are available for purchase or rent. See if they segment the list in different ways, such as geographic or demographic. Create a marketing piece to create leads based on the preferences of these various potential customers' location or age qualifications, and follow them up.

It's Easy as 1–2–3

Another approach is to target a particular neighborhood or business area that you desire. Obtain a mailing list from a reputable list company, and use it to create a marketing piece with a special offer and call to action. Develop a letter, postcard, and flyer around that offer. Send the letter to the homes or businesses in the area, and then after a week, distribute a flyer with the same offer in person. In the third week, send the postcard with the offering. By taking these steps, you are segmenting areas and targeting them at least three times. I would recommend coming back after a month and executing this one, two, three process all over again. The reason for this is what I call the *21 Times Approach*. You can market to a person, and it may take seven times before they even notice. It may take seven more times before they take any interest, and it may take seven *more* times before they are motivated enough or in the market to take action.

Wedding and Job Promotion Announcements

Many local newspapers and business guides have sections for special announcements. You can use the Internet to easily find the addresses that you need to send special congratulations, an offer, and even a gift. You are using reciprocation and obligation in this marketing strategy. For example, if you are a photographer, you might look for engagement announcements, and send a special report entitled "The 10 Most Common Mistakes Made by Couples When Planning Their Weddings." You can enclose a sales letter that offers another free report online, like "The 7 Secrets to Getting the Best Wedding Photos for the Least $," and offer a free surprise bonus just for getting the free report. When the customers go to the web site, they must enter their contact information to get the report and be able to collect the free surprise bonus offer. The bonus offer can be a discount for different packages or add on items included in package offerings. You now have identified them as a warm to hot lead, and can continue to market to them in multiple ways to create a relationship and identification with you. Here's a tip: Don't market to them just once. Keep marketing in a sequence. Eventually, you will convert a large percentage of these leads into customers. Even if you did not win them as customers for wedding photos, many of them could become customers in the future for some other type of photography.

eBay

A foolproof way to get attention is to take a product or service and market it on eBay. You can test marketing, pricing, and geographic advertising as well. I have seen people create successful businesses marketing items as big as automobiles on the Internet. One eBay auto dealer touts his cars in Florida as no-rust, low mileage cars. This dealer offers an extended service policy, guarantee, and financing through eBay. Instead of one picture of the vehicle, he takes thirty-five pictures and places them on the site with the story of himself, his business, how he operates, and the type of vehicles that he sells.

Pay-Per-Click

As a salesperson, you can use the pay-per-click method to sell your products or services in a low-cost way. If you use Google's Adwords or Word Tracker, you can search for keywords pertaining to your product, and find out what the bid is for these keywords and phrases. You can hit a gold mine when you being to search creatively. One of my clients, an automobile dealer, had us research pay-per-click as a marketing option. We typed in East (Name a town) Dodge. We found that there were a lot of searches for that keyword phrase; but there wasn't a dealership by that name. We quickly bid and won the phrase, and also bought the domain name for that title. We used a series of ads and landing pages to bring in a lot of low-cost leads. This is a strategy that can easily be used by an individual salesperson, as well as a business.

Multidimensional or Lumpy Mail

Everyone gets a ton of what is affectionately known as "junk mail." However, despite the often aggressive attitude that people have towards marketing-centered mail, you *can* use direct mail effectively. Instead of mailing to a random list, and sending your material to just anyone, *target* your list. Using factors like geographic, demographic, current owner, garage predictors, credit scores, and bankruptcies are just some of the ways to target. Next, instead of trying to send a letter that competes with everyone else, get creative. People tend to divide their mail into three categories.

A pile – The must-open type mail

B pile – The stuff that makes you think. You are not sure what it is, so you open it.

C pile – The junk mail that you automatically throw in the garbage.

Send multidimensional or lumpy mail to try to move up the food chain. Your mail will arrive in such a unique style that you stand a strong chance of getting it opened and reviewed. Here are some examples:

1. Wad up your marketing letter and enclose it in a larger envelope. Base your marketing and offer around the wadded up letter.
2. Trash can mailers
3. Wallet mailers
4. Coconut mailers
5. Bank bags
6. Boomerangs
7. Express mailers
8. Aspirin in air mail envelopes
9. Dynamite tube in a stick
10. Fortune cookie in a box
11. Tuxedo tube
12. Shredded money in a bag
13. Message in a bottle
14. Newspaper or magazine tear sheet mailers

(To view a sampling of the mailers above, go to www.lumpymail.com.)

Unique Business Cards

1. A million dollar bill with your picture in the middle and your unique message and contact information on the back.
2. Coins with your picture on the front and your contact info on the back.

3. Business cards utilizing pictures or caricatures. (Go to www.draw-me.com to see how you can get a professional caricature done, or have a bobble head doll made.)
4. CD-ROM Business Cards – Create your own digital business card. Google the term "CD ROM Business Cards" and you will find many suppliers.
5. Business cards with lead generation marketing – On the back, list a free special report and a website to go to get the report.
6. Poker Chip Business Cards.

Make News or Tie into the News

In his book *Purple Cow* (Portfolio, 2003), author Seth Godin talks about the ability to stand out from the crowd. The title comes from the idea that, obviously, a purple cow stands out from the rest of the cows. Mr. Godin also talks about the idea of *Buzz Marketing,* which puts forth the notion that in a cluttered world of marketing, it's best if your marketing creates a buzz. Your marketing should have the ability to spread virally. One way to do that as a salesperson is to create news or tie into current news stories

One of the marketing tactics that I employed while I was manager of the automobile dealership was to order a bunch of large blocks of ice. I placed a Toyota truck on the ice and held a contest for people to guess how long the ice would take to melt enough so that all four of the truck's tires would touch the ground. We had a camera and a timer to make sure of the time, and the winner received a trip to Hawaii. We made commercials and contacted every television and radio station, and newspaper in town. We received free publicity worth well over $100,000 for absolutely free. The contest caught newswires, and international sources contacted us. We sold a lot of vehicles and made a large profit from the promotion. The buzz from the promotion was strong and long—I had a *Purple Cow* promotion long before I had ever heard of the term. You might wonder: Can you do similar things as a salesperson on a limited budget? The answer is yes. You are only limited by your imagination. Awaken the P.T. Barnum inside of you.

A smart and persistent marketer will never go without leads or sales. You can supplement your need for great people skills with great marketing. Sales and marketing are not separate functions; to become a sales superstar, you must become a superstar marketer.

8

Dance With the One Who *Bought* You

Your Current Customers Are the Sexiest

Have you ever heard the expression "*Dance with the one who brought you?*" Most salespeople and businesses totally ignore this notion. They make a sale and then move on as quickly as possible. Although you *should* keep progressing after a sale, you must never forget about or neglect your existing customers. Here is a simple reality that, when acted upon, can make you rich: Your business should be largely based upon the customers that you already have. The really "big money" isn't out there among people you've never met. It's in your list of sold customers.

Salespeople tend to live by the rule of instant gratification. I have a somewhat crude term I created to describe this behavior: I call it being *instant-orgasmic*. Salespeople tend to want big results, and want them now—without too much work or "foreplay." That's okay; in fact, it's even the premise of this book. You can get results quickly by doing the things I share in this book. However, there are several things you can do that can increase your business right now—and most salespeople rarely do them. The reason that they avoid these tactics is because they involve utilizing your current customers. Most salespeople are myopic and short-term in their view of sales. They believe that their next dollar has to come from finding more new customers, or *"conquest customers."* One of the keys to becoming a sales superstar is keeping your customers, getting them to buy over and over, and finally, having them bring you more customers.

In the previous chapter I mentioned the five ways to increase your bottom line. Let's review them:

1. Sell more
2. Increase gross margins
3. Increase repeat sales
4. Increase the speed or cycle of your repeats
5. Create a continuity program

If you implement a game plan that focuses on numbers 3, 4, and 5, you will find that those steps will actually take care of getting numbers 1 and 2 done. Finding conquest customers will still be important; but the way that you obtain the majority of new customers will change—because your current customers will actually do much of this for you! By increasing your repeat sales and the speed of repeats, and by creating a continuity program of purchases, you will expand your sales numbers exponentially.

The industry in which I began my sales career—the automotive industry—is a perfect example of a market where salespeople tend to ignore the potential of their current customers. The average automobile dealership retains around 30 percent of its customers. The National Automobile Dealers Association has done research that shows that the average automobile dealer spends over $600 per vehicle on advertising. My own research shows that most (and sometimes all) of that money is spent on advertising for new customers. Many dealerships ignore their current customers. They hope those customers will come back, but the reality is that the majority don't.

Research also shows that the average dealership in the United States retains only 19 percent of their sold customers as customers for their service departments. The bottom line is that while the dealerships often spend small fortunes in trying to acquire new customers, they ignore their biggest opportunity—their sold customers.

When a dealership does not spend the time, effort, and money to build a relationship with customers, these customers don't come back. They forget about the dealership and don't feel any connection to it whatsoever. Without making a strong effort to convert the sold customers into clients for their service departments, the dealerships also lose the service business. The uncomfortable truth is that most dealerships have no one but themselves to blame for poor sales. Quick and convenient auto service businesses seized the opportunity to get those customers, and upstarts like Jiffy Lube are eating their lunch. That is a *huge* loss for a dealership. It's a proven fact that when customers buy and then service with the same dealership, the chances that they'll buy their next vehicle from that dealership goes up by 70 percent! Now that's a large leap. This pattern causes the Law of Familiarity to kick in. Since people create habits and patterns, most will continue to bring their car to a particular service department for repairs, even if they aren't necessarily thrilled with it—rather than having to change and go elsewhere for service Change equals pain for most people, so even a modest effort to keep a customer will pay off.

But what would happen if you put in more than just a modest effort? What if the average dealership spent a lot more of their time, effort, and money on creating a relationship with this sold customer? What if that dealership created VIP programs for its clients that gave them special privileges, services, and discounts, and designed a program around identifying and rewarding its best and most loyal customers? What if the dealership set up a personal relationship contact program? Do you think the average dealership could improve their service retention and sales retention numbers? Wouldn't this make a huge impact on the bottom line of the average dealership?

Now, whose job should it be to do all that? Salespeople like to blame management for their failure to institute the necessary programs for sales growth. But when these essential steps aren't taken, the ones who hurt the most are the salespeople. They lose repeat customers and referrals, which negatively affects current and future income. Repeat customers tend to pay higher gross margins than conquest customers; they pay for their comfort, and pay more often. In many businesses, the top 20 percent best customers make up the majority of sales or profits. As a salesperson, you can't wait for a business or employer to do this for you. Since it affects your income, *you* have to do it if management won't.

Failing to chase repeat customers carries significant consequences. Let's look at the manufacturers in the automotive industry—the so-called *"Big Three"*—General Motors, Ford, and Chrysler. I said so-called, because at the present time, Toyota has passed Ford and Chrysler and is on the heels of General Motors to be the overall sales leader. Meanwhile, Ford and Chrysler are falling like rocks. Although some people debate that trade, union, and political issues have contributed to their slide, the real reason is these companies built less reliable and less attractive vehicles for many years. Because Asian and European brands built better, more depend-able, and more striking vehicles, they were able to convert the customers of these American brands. Once customers have made a switch, they are less likely to go back. Therefore, it's much easier and much less costly to keep a current customer than to either get a new customer or try to win back lost customers. The original customers of the American brands must have experienced quite a bit of dissatisfaction to switch to the Asian and European brands. Unless they experience similar disappointment with the new brands, Ford, Chrysler, and General Motors will be hard pressed to switch them back to the *Big Three*.

What do these examples from the automotive industry have to do with you as a salesperson? The answer is *everything*. The same principles that applied with these salespeople and dealerships apply in your case. You have to have an active and determined game plan to get and keep your customers. You have to create ongoing relationships and use those relation-ships to grow your business. Let's discuss how you might do those things.

If a customer does not have some form of contact with you within a year after the sale is made, it is almost as though you never sold anything to them. You have neglected the relationship, and the customer probably doesn't even remember your name. To be sales superstar, you must follow up with your customers and create personal connections using as many media sources as possible. You must use all of the sources that you would use in general marketing and even a few more (since or if you have the customer's permission). A few are:

1. Letters
2. Postcards – Regular and oversized
3. Dimensional mail
4. Gifts
5. Personal calls
6. Voice messaging
7. Newsletters
8. Special emails
9. Auto responder emails
10. Referral programs
11. VIP memberships
12. Faxes
13. Personal visits if possible
14. Blogs
15. Instant messages
16. RSS feeders
17. Text messages
18. Video email
19. Frequent buyer programs

To rouse your thinking about customer relationships, let me tell you about a service that my own company provides auto dealers, which they use for their current and prospective customers. This VIP program provides a customer who buys a vehicle from the dealership a card that looks just like a credit card, and which entitles the holder to a discount on the service bill when they swipe it through a machine at the dealership. The card also rewards the customer with loyalty points that can be redeemed for future service, and in most cases, towards the purchase of a new vehicle.

The points are immediately recorded on a website, and the customer can keep track of them from home. The card also entitles the customer to products and services worth several thousands of dollars in value. Card-holding customers will receive emails, voicemails, text messages, letters, and coupons regularly that follow-up sales and service appointments. If the customer does not come in to the dealership for service within 90 days, communications are made with additional coupons and inducements. Our company has witnessed many dealerships double and triple customer retention rates with this program, and believe it or not—you and your company can accomplish many of these same things.

When you make a sale, you should develop a formal, written plan to communicate and establish a relationship with your customer. The following is an example of a schedule of items to send:

- 1 postcard a month
- 1 letter every 30 to 90 days
- 1 dimensional mail package every 3 to 4 months
- 2 gifts, coupons, or inducements a year
- 1 email per month
- 1 video email every 90 days
- 1 voice message or personal call every 90 days
- 1 newsletter per month
- VIP membership with continuity program
- Personal visits
- Periodic customer appreciation parties or events
- Recipe of the month – send a recipe of the month with a special offer, and watch how much response you get
- Periodic service or user clinics
- Promotional items with your name or contact information
- Informational articles
- Seasonal cards or offers – don't just think of Christmas, when everyone else sends a card! Think about the following:
  - Halloween
  - Valentines Day
  - April Fools gags

- Thanksgiving
- Groundhog day
- Tax day
- Earth day
- Secretary's day
- Holiday hangover in January
- Opening day for baseball
- Super Bowl Sunday
- Customers' birthdays
- Anniversary of purchase
- Create your own days – Favorite pet day, Call in sick day, and Come buy from us day

I have personally sent postcards with a picture of myself in a straight-jacket, skydiving, or with my kids. Don't be afraid that showing a more personal side of yourself will make you appear unprofessional, or that it will hurt your image. I've watched people in my marketing circles—doctors, lawyers, accountants, professional speakers, luxury product or service salespeople, dentists, business owners, real estate salespeople, and just about any field you can imagine—enjoy tremendous success using outrageous themes. Your customers will look forward to seeing the latest idea or promotion that you have come up with. They will begin to contact you and let you know how much they enjoyed your material, or how funny it was. Yes, you will occasionally hear from the curmudgeon who is upset that you sent something funny or outlandish. But you can't create your business around a few touchy people. If you contact enough people with emotional and original information, chances are that somebody will get mad—you can count on it. As a matter of fact, when you begin to do a good job with your marketing and customer relationship plans, you should hope that you upset or make at least one person cringe per day. This might sound a bit crazy, but when you tap into human emotions you get both positive and negative responses. The important thing is that you are getting responses. You can play it safe and be boring, and never get any business—or you can stop being so afraid of making someone mad every once in a while. Being boring is a critical marketing mistake. Here are some resources to help you to create a personal relationship contact program, and begin to automate much of it:

www.aweber.com – email sender with unlimited email and auto responder and RSS capabilities

www.lumpymail.com – dimensional mail service and product supplier

www.automaticresponse.com – voice messaging and 800 message lines (make sure to comply with all laws)

www.firststream.com – video email

www.nohasslenewsletters.com – no hassle newsletterswww.blifax.com – fax broadcasting (make sure to comply with all laws)

www.wordpress.com – free blogs and RSS feeders

www.myspace.com – social networking and blogs site

www.moreson.com – telephone conferencing

www.grandincentives.com – travel incentives

www.orientaltrading.com – premiums and gifts

www.internetvideoguy.com – video for web sites

www.internetaudioguy.com – audio for web sites

www.wallet-mailer.com – dimensional mail

www.mcmannisduplication.com – CD and DVD duplication

www.cityblueprint.com – printers

www.handymailing.com – mail house (800–624–3622)

www.sendoutcards.com – postcards

www.infusion.com – customer follow-up and marketing software

www.ezinequeen.com – shows you how to create and market through email and ezines

www.draw-me.com – email a picture and they will draw a caricature

To give you an example, here is a list of some of the relationship activities I've developed for my customers:

- Email newsletter once a month
- Auto responder emails set up to contact my customers every seven days with information and offers
- Video emails several times a year
- Postcard every month

- Dimensional mail to select clients several times a year
- Letters every other month
- Faxes to my business subscriber list every month
- 4 personal handwritten cards to different customers every day
- 10–30 phone calls to customers every day
- Monthly teleconferences
- Blog posts 1–4 times a month
- Family picture Christmas card
- Selected client personal visits, often with lunch or dinner
- Gifts and bonuses several times a year
- Special members-only section of your web site that provides discounts, freebies, and information
- Sending informational articles
- Other unique postcards for events and holidays
- I also write and publish several articles every month in trade magazines—as a salesperson, you should do the same. Customers respect expertise and being published gives you instant credibility. Use these articles in your marketing to new and existing customers.
- I use my caricature or picture on most of my marketing to generate a quasi-celebrity status

You might be wondering if there is a point when your customers get sick of hearing from you, or when you might face diminishing returns for your efforts. The answer is that generally, this does not happen. You can contact your customer with different media forms, and rarely overdo it. I have seen successful contact sequences that have over 130 contacts per year. I would invite you to push the envelope. Test your planned sequence to see what you can do. Usually, it's fear or laziness that keeps a salesperson from setting up a good contact sequence. Salespeople fear that their efforts will anger someone, and they usually fear doing what's necessary for a good relationship program. These fears tend to be unfounded, and all they do is allow an excuse not to try. Another common excuse is that your business or industry is different, or unique. In my experience consulting with businesses in many industries over several years, I have never found this to be true. It is a misperception or fear-based thinking every time.

Some of the things you should do in your follow-up program that most salespeople don't are to:

- Use humor
- Be outrageous, different, or unique
- Use multiple media
- Make you, your business, and staff quasi-celebrities
- Be politically incorrect
- Use plain language
- Use news or current events to tie into your message
- Concentrate on the message and the information more than the writing, spelling, or grammatical skills
- Use pictures
- Ask the customer to take action (maybe even to receive something or go to a web site or blog)

Avoid the Biggest Mistake in Customer Follow-up

Salespeople tend to get excited about creating a customer follow-up program. They start sending cards and letters and think that they're doing a great job. However, improper follow up can be damaging to your relationship with the customer. Most salespeople begin these programs by sending out generic cards and letters, and thinking that is sufficient. Your job is not to just to follow up with the customer, but to form a relationship that creates value, trust, and loyalty. Sending your customers generic, boring mailers actually causes them to feel disconnected from you. Go back to the idea of the A, B, and C mail piles, and imagine that you are sending mailers that start off with a greeting of "Dear Valued Customer." How valuable do you think they feel when they receive this impersonal communication? It's going in the garbage mail pile.

One of the smartest things anyone can ever do to become a superstar salesperson is to learn the craft of copywriting. Your ability to create emotional, exciting, and compelling copy will accomplish several things:

- It will teach you how to write things that people will read and take action upon.

- It will teach you how to apply those same principles to in-person selling.
- It allows you to create relationships, and not just contacts.

The power of the written and spoken word is amazing. If you take the time to learn and apply good copywriting skills, there will never be reason for you to be a broke and underperforming salesperson. I would invite you to read and learn all you can from the list of copywriter/marketers below.

Gary Halbert—www.thegaryhalbertletter.com
John Caples—www.caples.org
Ted Nicholas –www.tednicholas.com
Victor Schwab – How to Write a Good Advertisement (Wilshire Book Company, 1985)
Dan Kennedy – www.dankennedy.com
Jay Abraham – www.jayabraham.com
David Garfinkel – www.davidgarfinkel.com
Robert Bly – www.robertbly.com
Richard (Dick) Benson – Secrets of Successful Direct Mail (Bottom Line Books, 2005)
Gary Bencivenga – www.bencivengabullets.com
Claude Hopkins – My Life in Scientific Advertising (McGraw-Hill, 1st edition, 1966)
Joe Sugarman–www.psychologicaltriggers.com

More Examples of Multiplying the Wealth of Your Database

Let's say that you sell real estate. You can offer a yearly marketplace evaluation for the customers to whom you sell. Let your clients know where their house stands in the current economy, and keep them up-to-date on the marketplace. You can give a breakdown of:

- The total number of sales for comparable properties in the customer's area
- The average dollar amount of sale for comps in their area

- The average length of time on market to sell for comps in their area
- Best home owner tips for making a sale happen
- Market trends
- Geographic or neighborhood breakdowns
- Best selling property configurations
- Best property improvement tips
- The average marketplace evaluation for properties similar to theirs

The above statistics allow you to offer a more in-depth analysis. Ask the customer to contact you by phone, or have them go to your web site and fill out a questionnaire to get an immediate response. You can insert a short questionnaire or survey in the mailing so that you can give them the detailed examination that you've done. Then when they are ready to sell, you will be the first person they call. You will become a trusted advisor rather than a real estate sales agent. Why do this? To get the customer to take action. Any time you can get a customer to take action and go through a process, he commits to you and to the process. This creates a personal buy-in, and these action sequences also create a take-away mental close with the customer. This will makes him feel as though he has to qualify for something, and involves and connects him even more to what you are selling. If you create a relationship based upon value and providing information and expertise, you will be perceived in a different light than most salespeople. You will elevate your position and your trust factor.

Think Add-Ons and Continuity

Become a resource that provides value, and that customers can look to for information and to reduce or eliminate their problems. Think about added resources that can be promoted to the client as an upgrade or continuity program. Are there home services that can be bundled into a complete homeowners stress elimination package? Anything from a dog pooper scooper service (don't laugh—I actually had this service), to lawn maintenance, tree service, and more. You can put together a package that involves monthly fees for continual service. By taking these steps, you'll insulate yourself from down markets with a continual stream of cash, and you'll also bond with your customers. When a customer writes a check or makes a charge payment to you month after month, your value will be hardwired into that person's brain—and the overall process will reinforce your connection to the individual.

I've implemented a good number of these programs during my career in sales, but I've also experienced some as a customer. In my town of roughly 20,000 people, there are six coffee shops, and I go to one of those shops more than the rest—for three reasons. The first is that the owners and employees there are very customer–friendly, and have taken the time to get to know me and my family. Secondly, this shop has a very relaxing and comfortable atmosphere. And the third reason is that they have a coffee card which allows me to get my tenth purchase for free. I find myself getting my coffee card out before I get my money out, just so that I can get my free latte every tenth time I make a purchase. That little bit of continuity pulls me in and keeps me buying coffee, lunches, and gift cards from this same shop. Unfortunately, the customer-conscious owners have recently sold the coffee shop; and the new owners are not especially friendly. They have not asked me my name, or introduced themselves. They have a hard time completing a small transaction, and have now informed me that they are no longer accepting or giving out coffee cards. I felt rejected—and this is short-sighted stupidity by an ineffective business with dumb owners. They took a nice, inexpensive continuity and rewards program, sprinkled with good customer relations, and trashed it. As a result, they have lost me as a customer. My dissatisfaction in continuing to go there outweighs the pain of finding somewhere else to go. As a salesperson, you must never allow this happen. You have to fight tooth and nail for your customers. Sales superstars always do.

If you are employed by an agency, you may be thinking that doing these things would be difficult or even impossible. But when you start to think this way, you begin to fall into a trap called "mis-matching." This means that you consider ideas and immediately focus on those which don't easily match your own situation. You begin to discard these ideas, because you've already created reasons why it would be hard to implement these processes, or why they aren't readily doable using your first version of the idea. Sales superstars tend to be matchers—not mis-matchers. They look first at what *does* match up, and then try to fix the other pieces that don't. By using creative thinking, sales superstars often identify opportunity gaps, and then create business by filling these gaps. If you are not the entrepreneurial type, then create a proposal for your employer based upon your ideas. Show him or her how to make the idea work for your company, and how you can create and execute the idea for the employer—and receive a piece of the pie as well.

In addition, think of niches and opportunities that can be exploited. There is a rising-wealth class that will spend large amounts for products, services, and anything that provides exclusivity, comfort, convenience, and stress reduction. Create a customer retention program that provides an apples-to-oranges comparison of you and your competitors. Make your prospective customers consider the benefits and value they get from you before, during, and—just as importantly—after the sale. Your competitors are competing on a one dimensional and linear playing field, and it's your job to change this. For example—if someone was shopping for a product or service that you sell, what can you or your employer add as a bonus that keeps the customer from considering price only? Can you add to what the customer receives after the sale? When I was working as an independent leasing agent renting automobiles, I offered a sales service in which the customer never had to enter a dealership. I found the vehicle for him, and I arranged the lease through the best available source. I could also arrange a test drive at the customer's home or work. I delivered the vehicle, and did the paperwork right there. The services that I provided made the comparison of me to anyone else a comparison of apples to oranges. Providing assistance like this differentiates you from the masses and ties the customer to you. Taking such action brings you greater and even new revenue streams. Always think of the "*river of nickels*" theory.

How to Get Your Customers to Sell for You

Imagine that you are a boat salesperson. Boating enthusiasts tend to hang around with one another. They tend to know other boaters, and know which of their comrades might be in the market for a boat. In your sales, you have just taken a really nice boat in as a trade-in. You should immediately make two types of calls. The first is obviously to the list of potential clients looking for the type of boat you just acquired. Even if a customer is looking for a brand new boat, you can call and inform them about his one, and tout the substantial amount that they can save by buying a pre-owned boat. The second type of call you should make is to any current boat-owning customer that you have. You will call him and say the following:

"Hi, this Mark at Prestige Boats, how are you? Great! Am I reaching you at a good time today? The reason for my call is that we took in a beautiful boat in trade today that is_____" (give as much information as possible about details, benefits, and selling points of the boat). I am calling some of my preferred customers to let them know about the boat, because when we get a really nice trade-in like this one, it usually does not last long before it is sold. I wanted to let you know about it before the boat is ready for sale, so that I could give you the inside scoop before the other salespeople begin to sell it. You might not be in the market for another boat— but I wanted to ask you if you knew of any friends, family, co-workers, or fellow boaters that might want a really nice used boat like this before the general public finds out about it."

(Just a note on this technique: Some sales trainers suggest not asking the customer, "How are you?" for various reasons. But I have found that with the right voice inflection and enthusiasm, this phrase *does* help. Also, some sales trainers are against taking the curse off the call by inquiring, "Am I reaching you at a good time?" However, I have found that although you risk having the customer shoo you off the phone, if you use positive voice tone, inflection, and attitude, you will keep the customers on the phone and avoid upsetting the ones who might not allow you to talk to them. Keep in mind that sales trainers have *their way* of doing something. However, that does not mean that it is the *only* way to do something. You must try everything that you learn, and see what works best for you.)

People like to get a deal. They like to be in on a secret, or get the inside scoop, and they like to have a shot at what others can't get. And people really like special invitations. If you are don't believe me, just think about the crowds that go shopping at 5:00 AM the day after Thanksgiving.

Think about the car dealership that does invitation sales and has hundreds of people come in to visit in just one day. Remember the line by Michael Douglas in the movie *Wall Street?* "Greed is good." Greed has always been a strong motivator in sales and marketing. You are applying the principle of greed, somewhat, to create leads—and there is absolutely nothing wrong with that. You are helping your clients at the same time. I have seen many situations in which customers wound up buying a product that they were not originally in the market for. If nothing else, clients might try to assist you by suggesting an alternate buyer for the product—this allows them to help a friend, and look like a hero in the process—so make sure you reward them for doing so!

By using the principles I discussed in the previous chapter combined with the ideas in this chapter, it's possible for any salesperson to completely eliminate begging for customers. Automobile, boat, and RV salespeople can avoid standing on the showroom floor and praying for someone to show up. Real estate salespeople can avoid holding inane "open houses" that only produce about 3 percent of all home sales. Manufacturer sales reps can stop having to submit bids and pandering to be the low-cost bidder (and notice that I said bidder—not provider). Your goal is to do everything you can to eliminate your dependence on being a beggar salesperson. Keeping your customers and using them to grow your business is a huge key to being a sales superstar and achieving sales freedom.

9

The Yellow Brick Road and Its Potholes

The Pros and Cons of a Sales Process

There are two types of salespeople: those with a defined sales approach and those who I will refer to as the "*wing its*." The *wing its* want you to think that they are just "keeping it real." They tell you that each customer is different, and that you can't have a defined sales approach. The *wing its* just want to treat people right, and everything will be okay.

Here's the brutal truth about the *wing its;* they are usually either ashamed of being salespeople, or they are lazy. They are making excuses for being unprepared, and they're afraid of their customers. The *wing its* believe that they can sell successfully using their personality alone. The *wing its* are so afraid of having a "sales" persona attached to their names that they believe customers will buy if they want to—and if they don't, they won't,

135

and the salesperson can't make the ultimate difference. The *wing its* are order takers. And *wing its* make up over 95 percent of the salespeople in the world.

I am now going to make an unfair analogy, and compare salespeople to soldiers in battle. Now, I know that nothing should really be compared to soldiers or battle—but I believe you will get the point and understand that it is merely that—a comparison. Nothing to be taken at face value, so here we go . . . Although I have never been a soldier, I am pretty sure that soldiers spend most of their life training and preparing in every way possible for all imaginable scenarios that they could encounter. I don't believe any soldier wants to be on the battlefield with the enemy coming at him and be wondering, "Okay, what do I do now?" Because then the Sergeant has to tell the idiot, "Duck, dumb ass." That's exactly what managers of unprepared salespeople do every day. Bad managers accept and therefore promote unprepared behavior. Don't be one of the salespeople who neglect to prepare anything except excuses.

Obviously, salespeople don't die a physical death if they are not well prepared; they just feel like they are dying while they experience financial demise. As a salesperson, you must be prepared for all possible situations, and must attempt to follow a predetermined path. Yes, I realize that sales situations can go in any and all directions. However, to operate at peak performance, you must determine the course that you desire, and know how to get back on it should a customer wander off. You need to know and practice your *Yellow Brick Road to Sales Success*. However, you also need to understand that there are potholes in the road to the sale that can eat you alive.

Now, do I mean that you need to identify a well-defined process that you can use from the initial meet and greet, right through to the close and contract? YES! YES! and YES! You also need to make sure that your sales process is dramatically different from that of your competitors. Otherwise, your customer will lump you with all other salespeople. You must move the customer into cognitive disassociation, and help him to distinguish you immediately from everything else they have seen or heard from other salespeople. Your customer must see you as the only stand-out choice among "me too" type order takers.

Do you remember taking tests in school for which you were *really* prepared? You knew how you'd do, before you even took the test. You also knew what the result would be when you *weren't* prepared. The actual test was just a manifestation of your emotions and thoughts that led to the right or wrong behavior.

Competence equals confidence. Customers buy from confident salespeople. When was the last time you bought something from a salesperson and turned to your spouse and said, "Honey, I wanted to buy from this salesperson because he seemed really confused, unprepared, and totally incompetent." This does not happen. When you successfully prepare for all situations, your confidence rises significantly, and a customer can sense your confidence just as he would be able to sense your fear. This, in turn, gives the customer a significant boost in confidence. In traditional selling approaches, confidence is usually displayed as arrogance; the salesperson talks down to the customer and falls into the habit of telling versus asking and sharing. In my Contrarian selling method, you are sharing your expertise with potential clients in a manner that helps them make buying decisions.

All other things being equal, price will usually be the final decision point for the customer. Your job as a salesperson is to make other things *not* be equal. You must lower price on the price-value scale by increasing the value the customer gets from you and the product or service. Even if it's the product or service that the customer perceives to be superior, it will be your job as the salesperson to deliver the message. In the car business, there is a term to describe what criteria customers use to make a decision called, "Money, Me, or Machine." The bottom line is *the salesperson always makes the difference.*

I have been a professional speaker for many years. I used to do one-day sales seminars all over the country. The more I worked on my opening, material, delivery, humor, voice inflection, timing, and closing, the better my program became. Most importantly, the more I developed and practiced my talks, they became a more natural part of me and seemed less rehearsed. You must make your sales "speech" as natural a part of you as possible. You must become so familiar with what you say to potential customers that it never seems practiced or rehearsed—it should simply become a conversation. You must be able to insert each customer's information to tailor your presentation. Avoid one-size-fits-all canned sales spiels.

There are actually some surprising correlations between improvisational comedians and salespeople. I have had several conversations with improv comedians about what they do and how they do it, and have discovered some interesting points. If you've ever seen an improvisational act, you know that the troupe may ask for a word, idea, or movie as a starting point for the performance. One or two members begin, and each one builds onto what the last one has said or done. I always leave these shows amazed by the players' creativity, brilliance, and ability to think on their feet.

What you might not know about improvisation is that the players actually practice and rehearse. How do they practice such inventiveness? They imagine various possibilities, and then practice what they might do and all of the conceivable directions that the act could go in. They build up their improvisational muscles. They understand that the more you do something, the more it begins to hardwire your brain to consider what you've practiced a habit or pattern. You move to the level of "Unconscious Competence." You are now able to act in a manner that comes to you immediately and naturally. Improvisation can then occur freely because you've developed the confidence and mindset that allows your brilliance to naturally emerge.

The process of selling involves components that are almost identical to those of improvisation. As a salesperson, you can (and should) have a defined process. You can proactively plan for all potential doubts from a customer and directions that the sales process might take. You can even come up with a strategy to handle common objections before a customer voices them. Although each customer may be different and present varied scenarios, the patterns that they tend to present are surprisingly similar. You can boil down all of the potential paths that a sale might follow to just a few directions. You can classify all objections that you will ever hear into just a few categories. Therefore, you can easily prepare for all sales, as a form of "controlled chaos."

A few years ago, I was speaking at the National Automobile Dealers Association convention in Orlando, Florida. After the convention, I went swimming in the hotel pool with my son Jake. The pool had one of those long, winding slippy-slides that Jake and I love. You get up to the top, and you take off. You slide swiftly and effortlessly to the bottom. I would invite you to think of each step of your sales process as if going through one of these slides, and try to determine whether there is any part of your sales process that keeps the customer from moving smoothly and effortlessly to the end.

Try to pinpoint the exact point at which your customers typically disconnect from your process. Where do your customers tend lose interest, get upset, or begin to voice their objections? These areas are the roadblocks of the slippy-slide. The good news is that the traditional sales processes that most salespeople use never address roadblocks; they actually perpetuate the presence of these obstacles by clinging to the importance of the "standard process." The reason that this is good news for you is because you know that all you have to do to succeed is to be different. NEWSFLASH: If your process causes your customers to be uncomfortable, feel manipulated, or often raises objections—then it's time to change the process, or scrap it altogether.

Now Let's Discuss the Cons . . .

You know the pros to a using a good sales process—becoming proficient at recognizing customer patterns, identifying the usual roadblocks, and knowing your process at an "unconscious competence" level. Now let's discuss the cons. Most sales processes are inherently flawed. They usually have many steps or approaches that violate the "slippy-slide" effect. They introduce roadblocks for you as the salesperson and for the customer. One of the reasons that sales processes tend to be flawed is because many of them are outdated. Most were created when the idea of sales was what you saw in movies like *Tin Men* or *GlenGarry Glen Ross.*

Another reason that sales processes are flawed is due to the fact that they're often based upon manipulation, lying, strong arming, and forcing someone to buy. In fact, you often hear the word "control" to describe sales. You can strongly and masterfully guide, direct, and assist a customer, but your goal should *never* be to control the customer. Any attempt to wield power over a customer in this way sets in motion a cause and effect sequence that introduces conflict and discomfort. In effect, you are creating a customer who feels uncomfortable and generates a lot of spoken or unspoken objections. This is a prime example of the unintended consequences of a rigid sales process. Because of the flaws therein, a salesperson incites in the customer the exact opposite of the response that he had hoped for. In other words, he has planned his failure.

You must think like a Contrarian, as I discussed briefly in Chapter 3. The definition of Contrarian is someone who is, "opposed to, opposite in nature, or different." If you look around, you'll realize that most salespeople suck. Most salespeople are starving to death. Most salespeople are miserable, unhappy, hate their jobs, and are in a constant state of struggle. Do you really want to follow their example just because someone said that's the way you're supposed to do it?

Sales superstars break the rules—this is a fact. Sales superstars follow a process based upon TLC, which you know now is "Thinking Like a Customer." You must create a sales process imagining that you are a customer instead of a salesperson—and putting yourself in the position of the person being sold *to,* not the person selling. When I first got into sales, I was told to stop thinking like a customer and think like a salesperson. Horrible advice! Being empathetic to the customer's desires is one of the most essential characteristics of superstar salespeople. How can you identify with customers when your entire sales method is based upon your own thoughts and desires instead of theirs?

Don't get me wrong: I am not selling you a mushy, feel-good, "Kum Bah Ya" approach to selling. The customer is not always right; and yes, some customers *do* have to be guided, directed, and even pushed. Superstar salespeople are not afraid to emotionally and psychologically tilt the game in their favor. Make no mistake about it—it's your job and your mission. However, to do this correctly, you must start your sale from the customers perspective.

Traditional sales training teaches you to fail. It is a one-size-fits-all approach that causes salespeople to act like lemmings, which are little animals that follow each other off of a cliff, one by one, to their death.

You cannot let other salespeople lead you to your death; you must be different. Let's discuss how you can do that.

In the Beginning. . .

Get in the Door and in Position

If you are in a sales position that requires getting an appointment, don't follow the masses. Most salespeople are either going to cold call on the phone or cold call in person and ask for an appointment. If you are extremely talented and you practice this for many years, you can become good at it. But let me ask you, why would you work your butt off and beat your head against the wall day after day, year after year if you don't have to? Wouldn't you rather employ tactics that are both easier *and* more effective?

For many years, my company sold seminars the old-fashioned way. First, we would pick a city and a venue for the seminar. Next, we would begin to cold call a target audience of businesses. Our goal was to reach a decision maker and, in a short period time, convince them to let us give a free, 20 to 30 minute sales meeting for their staff. We touted the selling points for the meeting as being free, motivational, and educational. The sales staff would learn specific information that could help them sell something that very day. At the end of the meeting we would share information about my upcoming seminar, and sell tickets to anyone who was interested.

After many years of basically selling door-to-door in this fashion, and teaching many others to do the same, I became exceptional at it. I knew that I was as good as or better than anyone in world at this process. I made a ton of money being a road warrior. Although you might think that this would have made me happy—it didn't. The reason is because I knew that this was not a smart or efficient manner of selling. I also knew that the time I spent selling this program was limiting my growth. Spending all day panting and begging like a dog for a sell is not only a poor way to sell; it also tends to burn salespeople out and lower their self esteem. I wanted to add additional and more efficient ways to create sales.

Working *IN* the business all day was keeping me from working *ON* the business. The major shift in your success as a salesperson will be when you go—as I did—from spending the majority of your time working *in* the business, to working mostly *on* the business. Several things have to occur before you can make this change, though. As I discussed in Chapter 8, you must learn to market yourself efficiently. You have to learn how to automate your marketing, and you must use marketing that provides power and leverage. Making these initial changes will directly affect your ability to get customers, and will tweak the rest of your sales process in a positive manner. You will position yourself properly with the customer from the very beginning. Your customers will treat you as an invited, respected guest and a solution provider—versus a beggar and pest. You will see from the examples below how marketing is a part of your sales process.

You have to choreograph selling, performed at the highest level, with *power* and *leverage*. Your best sales are made when someone is buying, rather than being sold to. These two components create—at the very least—the perception that the customer should take action, make an appointment, or buy, and do it with you. You'll establish an environment that promotes a sense of urgency within the customer, who is buying, rather than being sold. People feel threatened when they are sold, and such a reaction induces the human brain's "fight or flight" mechanism. Yes—this aspect of sales truly draws upon an *actual* human, biological function.

You must utilize your power and leverage to get an appointment, and to do so you have to differentiate yourself from the pack of salespeople normally knocking on the door. Try the following methods, instead of traditional cold calling or appointment techniques, to begin your sales process.

Get Their Attention

Anything that is out of the ordinary will automatically command attention. For example, send a unique sales letter in a FedEx envelope to a potential customer. FedEx is a wise choice, because these packages are delivered to the intended party, and delivered immediately. This will ensure that a potential customer will open this letter and allow you to cut through the clutter and move immediately to the top of the pile. Using this tactic, however, is just step number one. You now must enclose within your package a sales letter that will get you an appointment or an opening to make your presentation—or, better yet, that will spur on the customer to take action and contact you.

As an attempt to get our targeted potential customers to sit up and take notice, our company once sent them a bank bag with *"I guarantee I can increase your bottom line by $100,000 in 60 days or I will pay you $10,000"* printed on the outside. We included inside the bag, along with the sales letter, a 100 Grand candy bar. This introduction got the decision makers' attention, and separated us from the crowd. The customers took the action that we wanted them to take. The mailer changed our status to invited guest, rather than one-size fits-all beggar. And although you may not be able to use that same type of headline or guarantee, with a little creativity and smart copywriting, you can be just as effective.

Once again, remember TLC—Think Like a Customer. Contemplate what you can provide to help that customer and maybe their business. Can you provide a potential lead? A marketing idea? Be specific. Everyone says they have a way to build sales and cut costs, but you must be explicit and give guarantees if possible. Make your guarantees real and truthful, and as mentioned in a previous chapter, use *the better than the money back guarantee.* Make the guarantee big, bold, shocking, and unique.

Don't make the mistake of worrying about the cost per mailing, or the cost per lead. These are concerns of small-minded salespeople. Your cost per mailing should be higher than what anyone would think of as normal. You don't want to be normal; you are looking for results, and so you need to be extraordinary. Don't worry about huge bulk mailings; start with small, measurable mailings whose results you can test. Your goal is to get sales—continual sales, and repeat sales—not to send a bunch of letters. Worry about results; not cost per mailing. Think about cost per sale. Think of the customer's dollar value to you. Think of the lifetime dollar value of the customer.

Use Unique Gifts or Presentations as Door Openers

You can tell the customers up front that you are shamelessly bribing them. Let them know why you are willing to risk the ridicule and rejection for doing so. For example, have gourmet pizzas delivered to the decision maker with a note: "Enjoy the pizzas as a gift from me, and be on the lookout for a special delivery in one hour." Then have a CD or DVD player delivered with a unique message, asking the decision maker to take the next step. It could be that you will be calling him at a certain time; or that you want him to call a toll-free hotline for a free recorded message that, at the end, asks the caller to email or call you, or take your call.

I can recall one instance where I was having a hard time getting to see the decision maker of a company that I had targeted. So I went to a cookie store and had a huge custom cookie made for him that had a picture of a foot and said: "How do I get my foot in the door?" I attached my business card with contact information to it. The next day, I received a call from the decision maker of the company, who invited me in to speak at their sales meeting. We had an awesome, energized meeting. The decision maker loved my information, and paid for his entire sales staff—from three different businesses—to attend my seminar. Ninety-five percent of salespeople would have just made one attempt, and then quit. They would not have taken the time to think of a unique solution to the problem, or an original way to introduce themselves; they simply would have accepted defeat. You can't worry about potential negative responses. We live in an uptight and politically correct world, and you're bound to offend somebody at some point. The only way to avoid this is to do nothing at all, which is certainly not an option. Stop worrying about what the masses think—the masses are rarely, if ever, right.

You Are Reading This Book as a Result of These Ideas

I was told repeatedly by authors and publishing experts that a major New York publisher would not publish a sales book by a first-time author, and would definitely not look twice at a proposal without an agent. Lo and behold, you are currently reading a book written by a first time author, and published by a major New York area publisher. How did I do this? First, I made a list of major business book publishers. Secondly, I did research to find out who the editors were for each publisher, and then I made a plan to place myself physically in front of one of the editors. It took attending a conference in Cancun, Mexico to do this. I engaged the editor in a one-on-one conversation, and planted a seed about my book idea. Later, I emailed the editor with my book proposal idea, and asked if I could submit the proposal to him. The editor said yes, and I was eventually offered a contract and advance for the very book that you are reading.

The experts were right about the difficulty that a first time author faces in getting the attention of a major publisher. They were right about the fact that it's extremely rare for a publisher to look at a book proposal without an agent. The experts are wrong, however, that it can't be done. With great positioning and enough determination, you can get in front of the decision makers.

Write and Then Write Some More

Part of being an effective speaker is learning to be an effective writer, and to do this, you need to hone your skills. Offer to write a guest column for your local newspaper on sales or customer service. Offer to write for trade magazines that your customers read. Being published positions you as an expert, so don't give me the excuse that you can't write. Just write. If you need, get someone to help you. There are tons of editors, ghostwriters, and English teachers that can help you. People are looking for information and help—not grammar teachers. The people who will complain about your writing won't be your buyers anyway, because those people are too busy worrying about things that don't matter in their business. At the end of your article, ask to have a byline with your contact information. If the publication will allow, also add free tips or a free special report that customers can email, call, or go online to get by giving their contact information.

Every month, I write and publish three to five articles in trade magazines to my target audiences. People read the columns and then call or email me—so I know that this is paying off! This marketing approach provides me with business, and positions me as an expert. The customer is contacting *me,* which grants me immediate leverage and power. One of these customers is better than a hundred cold customers. You must turn the game around, and go from trying to knock the door down to being invited inside.

Meet and Greet

Let's shift gears and talk about the meet and greet from the perspective of a retail salesperson. I was fortunate enough during my time at the automobile dealership to have a veteran and knowledgeable sales staff that did very well. However, I always wanted to improve; so I began a mission to really observe, evaluate, and possibly advance our sales process. I started with the beginning of the sales process, which is the meet and greet. I watched our salespeople using the traditional meet and greet, by extending a hand and saying, "Hi, welcome to our dealership, my name is Joe Salesman, and your name is? What can I assist you with today?"

This greeting—although not what I'd prefer—is lot better than many I have witnessed, like the one I call the Texas greeting, "Can I hep ya?" (Don't get mad Texans, you know it's true. I started selling in Texas so I am fond of you anyway.) I think the traditional meet and greet contains a lot mistakes and often accomplishes the opposite of what it intends. Let's break it down. First of all, 98 percent of the time the customer responds to the traditional greetings by saying, "I'm just looking and shopping around right now; if you give me your card, I will come get you if I need you."

The traditional meet and greet immediately incites the, "I'm just looking" defensive reply. Now you are fighting an automatic objection, right from the start. You are already going uphill in this sales process. If this happens 98 percent of the time, then why do it? Remember the slippy-slide. Don't create roadblocks.

Secondly, the act of extending the hand for a handshake to welcome the customer is a custom that is rooted in misinformation. Many people don't want to shake your hand at that point. Shaking hands makes people feel awkward and would be a taboo in some cultures. And shaking hands with a female would be a taboo at *anytime* in some cultures.

Exchanging names at a point that is meant to be the beginning of relationship building is usually an exercise in futility that will actually hinder your rapport with the customer. I found that our sales staff almost always forgot the customers' names, and the customers often did not remember theirs, either. Picture greeting your customer in this way, and then dropping hands at the end of the handshake. Something drops to the floor—what is it? The answer is the names you just exchanged. What would be the one simple thing you could do to break barriers, build a connection, and form a personal bond? Hearing, remembering, and using your customer's name.

Here's a unique meet and greet method that eliminates the problems created by more traditional techniques. Try being proactive in your approach, and draw upon the customer's usual response before he or she can use it. "Hi folks, welcome to ABC business, are you out today to begin to look and shop around?" What is the customer going to say—"No, I'm just looking and shopping?" Of course not—you took the defensive response away by stating it first.

You have expressed to them through your greeting that it is okay to look and shop. You are breaking down barriers by speaking in the customer's language. Your opening is what I call a Universal Truth Statement. *Of course* the customer is looking and shopping. This statement is something with which he can agree, and one that won't intimidate him.

Let's address something I call Proxemics in the meet and greet. Don't look for this term in your dictionary, because it's not there. I define Proxemics as the relationship of physical distance among people. There are three zones: The Personal Zone, which is roughly arms length; The Social Zone which is three to five feet away; and the Public Zone which is beyond five feet.

In a traditional meet and greet, you offer your hand, and therefore immediately enter into the customer's personal zone. In the United States and in many other cultures, such a gesture can cause quite a bit of discomfort for the person on the receiving end. The proper way to greet is to use the phrase I gave you more quickly. As you approach the customer, stop short, and stay in the social zone. Don't extend a hand unless the customer does. Then, after you use the "Just Looking" question, wait for the reply and play off the customer's response. Begin to ask the customer simple questions about what they are looking for. Too many salespeople launch into questions about financial matters, and nearly scare the customer to death. (We will address money issues in detail later on in the book; but it's best not to begin with this topic right off the bat.)

Now is a good time to take a step back and ask the customer to share with you what he or she is looking for, "so that I can guide you in the right direction to save time, and let you know what's on sale to save you some money." Bingo! Two buzz phrases you need to use over and over— *Save time and save money;* because universally, everyone wants to do these two things. And by taking that step back, you established tangible distance that probably helped the customer feel even more at ease.

After you have engaged the customer for a while, the hope is that he will soon begin asking you questions and giving positive signals—like making eye contact and physically moving towards you. Now you can begin the name and handshake sequence, using the theories of Reciprocity and Obligation. Remember that all this means is that you give enough to someone so that this person will feel obligated to give back, or reciprocate. It is as simple as the lessons you learned in kindergarten and Sunday School. You can even start off by saying that you are sorry, as in, "I'm sorry, I did not mean to rude—but I don't think I gave you my name, or that I even got yours. My name is Mark—and your name is . . . ?" Extend your hand and shake hands if the customer extends his to you. When doing so, remember this acronym.

CARS –   **C**oncentrate
              Attend to
              Respond and **R**epeat
              Save

You should *concentrate* on getting the customer's name, and *attend to* the customer's words and face. You can *respond by repeating* the name several times in your conversation. If you remember his or her name for 15 seconds, chances are that you will remember the name for the long-term.

Now that you understand the mechanics of a proper meet and greet, let's back up and talk about the mental components of this initial step in the sales process. What is going on in your mind may end up being more important than the actions; because if you don't have the mental part down, it won't matter what your mouth and body do. Salespeople tend to carry the weight of the world on their shoulders. If you have not sold anything in a while, it clearly shows in your body language and your voice. Zig Ziglar has a saying: "Give yourself a check up from the neck up." The saying that I have is somewhat different: "Put some slide in your glide and put some pep in your step." In other words, make your actions positive—and your emotions will follow.

Before you greet a customer, you must wipe the board clean in your mind. The past does not have to be indicative of the future. You must put a smile on your face, and as I directed before, say "showtime" loudly; because it's showtime for you and your customer. A potential client does not care that you have bills to pay, a nagging spouse, or any other personal problems. The customer tunes into the oldest radio station on earth—WIIFM—What's In It for Me? So, when you say "showtime," you remind yourself that the customers' priorities come first, and it's your job to get them what they want. You re-anchor your body and your mind to a more positive state. Say the word "showtime" right now, and tell me if it's even possible to have a frown on your face. The word ends with your mouth turned upwards.

I have seen many salespeople greet customers sounding as though they were at their own funeral. They've been hunched over and speaking without any enthusiasm, and do not even realize it. You must have an anchoring system to clean your mental "slate" and bring you back to a better selling mind frame. You can even close your eyes for a second, and see the few last customers to whom you made a successful sale. See the expressions on their faces, and picture them agreeing and signing. Consider the acronym WYSIWYG—"What You See Is What You Get." It's true—don't dismiss this as pop psychology. It's an undeniable fact that what you think about becoming, you become. The customer's initial perception of you can easily become reality in their minds, so you must use everything you that can to shift that perception in your favor. How a customer observes you is fundamentally *your* choice.

The way that you dress and groom yourself can make a big difference in this initial impression. When I am greeted by a salesperson that looks sloppy, I instantly dismiss the person in my mind. I immediately ask myself, "If he can't take care of himself, how can he take care of me?" Although casual dress has become the norm in the work world, I believe that the "dress down" culture of salespeople has further impaired the image and chances of selling in most situations. Try dressing more formally than your customers, and they will respect you and perceive you as someone who is different. Don't make the excuses the rest of the salespeople make. Make a commitment to excellence, beginning with your appearance.

For many years while I was selling my seminars, I would crawl in and out of cars all day long to see customers. The temperatures in which I worked ranged from blazing hot to freezing cold. But no matter the climate, I never let it interfere with my appearance. I was once asked by a sales trainee if it was necessary to put on his suit jacket when we got out of the car, since the temperature that day was in the high 90s. I answered yes. When he asked why, my answer was: "commitment." I was committed to looking better and making a sharper impression than anyone else that had ever called on that company.

Every day, there are salespeople all over the world calling on customers in clothes that fit poorly, that aren't ironed, and that look sloppy. Their lack of self-care shows disregard for a commitment to excellence. When I first started in sales, I was poor and really did not have the clothes that I needed. But I made sure to put away a large portion of each commission towards the purchase of new clothes. I knew that my clothes—just like a computer, a brochure, or a car—were tools to be used wisely during the sales process. They are assets to selling, just like anything else.

However, clothes aren't the only element in making a positive first impression. For those of you who are smokers, I would strongly recommend that you either quit or learn to disguise it. I can't tell you how many times I have had a salesperson approach me reeking of smoke and cigarette breath. These salespeople always lose me as a potential customer immediately. If I can't stand to be near you, then I can't buy from you.

Whenever you read a book, watch a movie, see a play or a comedian, you are greatly influenced by the beginning of the story or performance. If the opening is weak, your view will be clouded—no matter what occurs after. The outset creates an expectation for everything else that occurs thereafter. Either it catches your interest, or it doesn't—and the same is true for your sales process. The beginning is way too important to be anything less than spectacular.

There is an old saying that claims that "You don't get a second chance to make a good first impression." This phrase is powerful and true. Your beginning often dictates your middle and your end. Plan your beginning as though it is your only chance to make an impression—and you'll make certain that it won't be.

10
Setting the Stage

Earlier in the book, I talked about some of the usual pitfalls and objections you may hear as a salesperson. If you're proactive and set the stage to address and eliminate these pitfalls before they occur, then you'll be in good shape. Ignoring the risks and hoping for the best won't work. I often say that, "You can't sweep crap under the rug and expect the stink to go away." Traditional sales training has centered on avoiding the issues of price, or any other thorny topic. I believe you must address these matters immediately, before the customer brings them up.

By doing so, you've taken the necessary steps to frame the conversation yourself. You are guiding the customers in a direction with which they will be comfortable, and one that will also endear you to them—because of your honesty and unique process. I am clearly not telling you to walk into a sales situation, and give your potential client the lowest possible price up front. What I *am* saying is to address the issue of price and how it will be handled early in the process.

If you can give customers a beginning, tell them what the end looks like, and outline the path to get there, they will comfortably fill in the remaining details. Their minds will lead them to the destination as YOU have laid it out for them. *Make note of the following:* Customers fear the unknown. Left unaddressed, their fears will grow to levels that will render them unable to buy.

There are sales methods still taught today by so-called sales "gurus" that instruct salespeople to avoid price questions by using complete *bypass techniques.* These trainers tell salespeople to respond to questions about price by asking, "Who is going to be the lucky one to drive this vehicle home?" or, "Don't worry about price, let's make sure the product or service is right." Trainers advocate these methods as being, like the commercial says, "So easy, even a cave man can do it." The reality is when you use these phrases you sound like a cave man, and you're using techniques that are practically prehistoric. Customers today have high BS detectors. Certain procedures and word tracks that we talk about can help you; but you can't use any language that treats people like idiots. Remember, these modes of selling are so old, and have been taught and copied so many times, that *most* salespeople are still using them. Imagine what these lines sound like to a customer who has heard them a gazillion times before.

Job Mission

I believe in giving my customers something that I call a Job Mission. A Job Mission is dramatically different from the goofy corporate or company mission statements that authors and consultants tout. You know—the stupid plaques on office walls that all say the same syrupy mush that customers never look at, and wouldn't believe anyway, even if anyone in the company could remember to spout it (which, by the way, nobody ever can). I am talking about telling the customer in a quick and meaningful way, at the outset of the sales process, what I want to do for that individual, and what that situation looks like. For example: "Mr. Customer, my job is pretty simple. I try to help you get the product or service that you want, answer and address any questions that you may have, and help to make this fit into a budget with which you feel comfortable. Fair enough? Great! Let me give you a quick run down of what that looks like; and then, if you want to do it differently, or if the solution doesn't work for you just let me know. We'll tailor it to your needs, and it will be like the Burger King slogan—we will do it your way. Does that sound good?"

Although this particular technique is one with which I feel comfortable, you have to use your own words and your own style. Don't be robotic. People buy from people, not sales machines who spit out word tracks that sound like canned telemarketing pitches. The main ideas to address are the message and the customer's fears. Look at it this way: The customer only has so many questions they can ask, or matters about which they can be uncomfortable with. And as we've already learned, these things usually revolve around money, me, or the machine (product); and are— more often than not—easily addressed and fixed.

Moving Smoothly from the Greeting to Profiling

After you meet and greet your customer, you'll begin a dialogue that involves asking simple questions. Make sure that these are not too deep or scary, or questions that move the customer too far along in the buying path too rapidly. You always want to start with smaller, less invasive queries in your sales sequence, and then move to larger questions that stimulate more detailed responses. You might, for example, ask your customer the following:

1. "Are you looking for basic, medium, or well-equipped options?"
2. "Are you looking for lighter or darker colors?"
3. "Are you looking for a bigger or smaller house?"
4. "Are you looking for basic or comprehensive coverage?"

These serve not only as profile questions, but also as transition inquiries. They are "getting to know each other" type of questions that reposition your rapport with the customer. They move you toward communicating with one another, creating a relationship, and reducing the awkward "Us vs. The Mean Salesperson" mentality.

Once you begin a conversation and have spent a little time with the customer, you can shift to asking deeper profiling questions that will lead to a presentation or demonstration. To make this transition go more smoothly, you can wisely use what I call *"Universal Truth Statements/Questions."* I give them this title because they are positive statements or questions and almost impossible for anyone to disagree with, such as:

1. "With your permission/if you would *allow* me to, I could share some the sale specials with you."
2. "With your *approval,* I could let you know about some of the products/services that we have on sale."
3. "If it's *okay* with you, I can share with you some of the products/services that we have special values on"
4. "Can I take a minute to show you something really neat about the product/service that you are looking at?"
5. "Would you like to hear the number one reason why most of our customers buy this product/service?"

What customer is going to say, "Please don't show me the sale/special/value product or service?" It is an almost universal truth that everyone wants to save money and save time. These are both extremely valuable currencies; therefore, you should use the terms "save time" and "save money" throughout the sales process. As you continue to anchor these phrases into the customers' conscious and subconscious minds, they will begin to perceive the benefits of your ability to save them time and money. Remember that perception is reality. I am certainly not asking you to manipulate or lie to sell anything, but the reality is that you must guide and direct your customers' perceptions. This is why it's called selling instead of giving.

A prime example of this is my favorite place to eat, Jeff Ruby's Waterfront Restaurant. This establishment sits on the Ohio River and provides an amazing view of the beautiful Cincinnati skyline. The food and service are as good as it gets. Jeff Ruby, the restaurant's owner, is known as a demanding entrepreneur who trains his people well—and it shows. Every part of the dining experience at all of his establishments—food, staff, and ambience—is consistently impressive.

I remember a time that I took a group of my customers, who were visiting from out of town, to the Waterfront for dinner. When we arrived at the restaurant, I went to the restroom. As I finished washing up, a smiling attendant handed me a towel and said, "It's a nice place, isn't it?" I replied that it was. Awhile later, after a long dinner, I went back to the restroom. As I was washing my hands once again, the same smiling attendant handed me a towel and said to me with even more vigor, "Sure is a nice place, isn't it?" And I replied, with even more vigor than the first time, that it sure was a nice place. I raved about the view, the food, and the service.

I stayed with my guests at the restaurant for a few post-dinner drinks, and talked business. After a long night, I hit the restroom one more time before we took a cab back to the hotel where my guests were staying. Once again, as I was finishing washing my hands, the attendant handed me a towel and before he could even open his mouth, I found myself telling the attendant in a loud and exuberant voice, "Man, this is a nice place, isn't it?"

Now, think about my experience for a second. The attendant repeatedly proclaimed to me, and I'm sure to the other guests, "Nice place, isn't it?" He was positioning everyone's point of view as they left the restroom and reentered the restaurant. Did this behavior influence the clients' perception? You bet it did! The attendant certainly wasn't saying "Hey, watch the fish, it sucks and it'll kill ya!"

I can't tell you if Jeff Ruby, or this particular employee's manager, taught the attendant to use this positioning phrase; however, I do know that every time I have had a meal at any Jeff Ruby restaurant, I have witnessed similar behavior by all of the employees. Jeff's staff helps the customers define their dining reality. Just like a placebo, I have no doubt that their comments and attitude influence the entire dining experience, including the guests' opinion of the quality of the food.

Remember: the best price, value, or special is a perception. Everyone's view of what makes up that so-called "great deal" is different. Does your use of those phrases and terms previously stated mean that you have to deeply discount your product or service? The answer is absolutely not. In my experience, there is no corollary between price and customer satisfaction. As a matter of fact, consider your own customers; you are apt to see that the happiest ones are those who pay you the most. And who are the most miserable customers you have? You got it—the ones who beat you to death on price, keep asking for freebies, and are never satisfied.

Here is something to remember: *"You must choose your customers just as they choose you."* Until you wholeheartedly believe, endorse, and live by this mantra, you will always be the beggar or unwelcome salesperson. When you make the mental shift from beggar to that of a value provider for your customer, you will become exponentially more attractive. You will create a position of power that boosts your message and the customer's perception of that message. When you implement the practices that I've outlined, you will experience a smoother transition into the rest of the sales process. You will undergo a shift in the environment you have created from that of the *usual* sales environment; and you will enjoy a better and more productive relationship with your customers.

Profile vs. Qualifying

Traditional sales training teaches you to ask qualifying questions. From a customer's perspective, I get pissed off just *knowing* someone wants to qualify me. Questions like, "How much do you want to pay?" "How much money do you want to put down?" "What size of an order are you looking to make?" are not only offensive, but paint you as the salesperson into a corner that you might not be able to get out of. By trying to be smart, you may be creating shoppers and losing customers. You can get all the information you want by asking smarter and less invasive questions. Some of these simply need to be dropped altogether—because all they are doing is taking you out of the game mentally.

I've experienced similar situations during my years as general manager of the automobile dealership. One Saturday, I had a sales manager who was out sick. As luck would have it, we were very busy that day, and I was left to coach the salespeople on all of their customers and deals. Our very best salesperson was Earl. Earl was all smiles. He could talk to just about anyone and create a relationship that almost always resulted in sales. Earl had a great attitude and it showed, even when he was only presenting a proposal to me as the manager.

This particular busy Saturday, Earl must have come into my office five times with proposals for car deals. He would tell me excitedly each time something along the lines of: "Hey Boss, I have a great couple here. They've picked out a new vehicle, they've driven it, and they love it. And that's not all—they bought their current vehicle from us, they service it with us, and they love us. They want to see our figures including payments and terms, and maybe a lease option as well." Reflect upon the way in which Earl presented this proposal. Everything was positive—the customers' previous experience with us, their consistent loyalty, and their current impression of the product that we were offering to them.

On the other side of the coin was a salesperson named Dick. Dick had been a good salesperson for many years, but was currently on somewhat of a downward slope. Dick came to me several times for coaching that Saturday with presentations that were dramatically different from Earl's. He would walk up with his head in his hand and begin to grumble, "I have this Internet guru out here. He wants prices and payments on several vehicles, but he won't drive any of them. He wants to be at $200–$250 per month on his payments with no money down. This guy says he definitely won't buy today; he is going to shop all over town for the best deal and he just wants our lowest price. He has figures from four different guides on his trade-in, and wants top dollar for it; but he owes more than what it is worth. Oh, by the way, he didn't bring his trade-in, and his wife didn't come—and she has to see the car before he buys." All the while, you could see Dick's face getting redder and redder as he was getting madder and madder. Eventually, he would blow up, raise his voice and say, "I'm not wasting all day with this guy. Do you want to talk with him or not before I get rid of him?" Towards the end of the day, Dick came shuffling across the showroom floor towards my office with his head down, a scowl on his face, and a deal proposal in his hand. All I could think was, "Dead man walking." I stopped Dick half way across the showroom and with my head in my hands asked, "What'd ya got Dick? I bet this deal stinks doesn't it? Get this guy out of here; we're closing in ten minutes."

A short while later I was driving home, thinking about my day. I recalled Dick and his last customer, and started laughing so hard that I had to pull over. The reason why? I had allowed Dick to program me into believing that his last customer was a bad deal that I needed to get rid of. The trouble was that I had never even *met* Dick's customer. I had never even seen him.

I had never read a deal proposal, seen a credit report, or gotten to look at his trade in. I had not seen anything. The truth of the matter was that Dick had programmed me to accept as truth that every deal he ever brought to my attention would be bad—so bad that I wanted to throw in the towel, go home, and dial 1-800-Kevorkian. Slitting my wrists almost would have been more pleasurable than working a deal with Dick.

Let's break this down. As a manager, I allowed Dick to ask qualifying questions such as, "How much do you want to pay?" "How much do you want for your payments?" "How much do you want for your trade?" "How much do you owe on your trade-in?" "Do you want to buy today?" All of these questions are money-centered questions that are based upon qualifying someone financially. They have nothing to do with the customer's wants, needs, desires, thoughts, or feelings. Even worse, all of the questions that Dick asked had negativity built right into them. Many of them also encouraged untrue answers that would put Dick behind the eight ball from the start. The responses to these so-called "qualifying questions" actually kept the customer from buying, and often led them to believe that they would have to shop elsewhere. The questions and the attitude that Dick used even influenced *my* perception of the customers. Worse yet, I allowed the negativity to influence my behavior. If someone tells you it's going to rain enough times, you begin to look at the sky and see clouds.

I came up with a few tongue and cheek sayings for qualifying questions in the automobile business. The Eleventh Commandment is, "Thou shall not pay more than $200–$250 for an automobile." The Twelfth commandment is, "Thou shall not put any money down." The Thirteenth commandment is, "Thou shall not buy today." In a Monday morning sales meeting, I laughed as I told all the salespeople that they no longer had to share with me the answers to the normal qualifying questions, because I already knew that the answers would be universally the same. Think about it, how many people are going to say, "Yes I want to buy right now, I am ready." Most people are scared. Their right to walk away is their power. When asked what they want to pay per month or how much they want to pay, most people will low ball you—because they want to protect themselves.

In essence, these questions are ridiculous—because they elicit answers that are wrong, defensive, negative, and that box you into working backwards financially. They cause conflict, heightened negotiations, and hard feelings. They have nothing to do with TLC—Thinking Like a Customer. The questions seek to qualify rather than profile.

Although people might argue that profiling is a bad thing in police work, in sales, profiling is positive and necessary. I want you to assume that all people qualify; and if not, it's your job to get them to qualify. Let's address the customer and let the finances fall where they may. There is an old baseball saying: "Just hit the ball and let it worry about where it goes." When you profile customers instead of qualifying them, you are taking a complete approach based upon helping the customer—not just making a commission.

The good news is that asking questions *correctly* can get you all the information you desire without the negatives that tend to come with the qualifying process. Instead of asking a customer what budgets or prices they want, ask him what his current budget is, or what he paid for this product/service the last time he bought. This will prevent the customer from feeling like he has to lie to you to protect himself, and will allow you both to deal in reality. You can work with what is known rather than what is unknown.

Asking people for current or past information tends to invoke the "Law of Familiarity." People are inclined to follow patterns that they are familiar with. If someone who currently owns a boat is looking to buy another one, you can ask about their current payments on the boat. You can then show this person a proposal on a new boat with an option that has enough of a down payment to keep overall payments comparable. Taking this step has allowed you to shift the burden of crafting a comfortable payment schedule to the customer. If the payments are too high, the customer can: 1.) put more cash investment, 2.) take a longer loan term, 3.) look at a boat with fewer features, 4.) look at a used boat, or 5.) look at lease options, if they are available.

Keep in mind when asking about current or past financial data that the main goal is to avoid scaring or offending the customer. You are simply showing concern for him and for his fiscal situation. You are dealing with the reality of the "knowns."

Some additional profile questions are:

- "Who will be the primary user of the product/service? Are there any secondary users?"
- "What do you like most about this product/service?"
- "Have you done anything to your current product that has increased the value of it?"
- "Other than price, what is the most important thing to you when you buy/purchase?"
- "Are you going to use the product or service for work or pleasure?"
- "Where do you work/Do you work close by?"
- "What do you do for a living?"
- "How long have you been in that field?"
- "How did you decide to get into that field?"
- "Are you considering purchasing any other products/services at this time?"
- "Is there anything that you would like to avoid in the process of looking and shopping for this product/service?"
- "Do you want to look at or consider other models/services if there are more savings?"
- "Can I show you figures with and without trading your current model?"
- "Are you considering the same price range this time?"
- "Are you looking for a product with basic, medium, or lots of features/services?"

Deal-Killer Questions

Earlier, we addressed some questions that create traps for salespeople—such as the following "Deal-Killer Questions" to avoid.

1. "Are you looking to buy today?"
   This question invites a false answer. Assume that everyone will buy until they give you reason to not believe it. Most sales are closed on the first attempt.

2. "What budgets/payments do you want to pay?"
   This will elicit a low-ball response and create a situation whereby the customer must lie to you to do business.

3. "What cash investments or down payments do you want to make?"
   You are provoking a low-ball answer, and are potentially scaring customers who lack capital or might be embarrassed.

4. "What color do you want?"
   Murphy's Law—They will want the only color that you don't have. Instead, ask if they are looking for lighter or darker colors. Show them something you have.

5. "What equipment do you want?"
   Murphy's Law—Again, they will ask for equipment that's out of stock or that you don't have. Instead, ask them more generic questions: "Are you looking for basic, medium, or lots of features?"

6. "What price are you looking for?"
   As with questions 2 and 3, you are inviting a low-ball answer. Instead, quote the price for your product or service, and start from your figure, not the customers.'

7. "If this is not the price/budget, what were you thinking instead?"
   The customer will either low-ball you here, or tell you that *you* are the salesperson and *you* should tell them. You have created what I call the yo-yo or back and forth part of negotiating, which customers hate.

8. "Are you sure we are comparing apples to apples?"
   You might ask this question when a customer tells you that someone else has your price or proposal beat by a mile. I have never heard a customer correct themselves and say, "You know, you're right. Your product/proposal has a ton more features or benefits. Yours *is* better." The customer will always say, "It's exactly the same, theirs has even more. It even has a rocket engine too. Yeah, that's

the ticket." Just call their bluff by saying the following, "Price will never be the final decision with us. I am sure we will find the difference." It's amazing how often the supposed huge price advantage of the competitor magically disappears when you make such a statement.

9. "Are you satisfied with your vendor/supplier/current source?"
    You are playing a weak game here. Most people will say yes, even if they don't like their current source, because they don't want to admit their mistake. You must allow the customer to save face. Offer your company or products with SDP—Specific Defining Proposition. Let the customer know what makes you, your company, and your product or service different, better, and unique. Ask questions to find out what is the customer's pain. Fix that pain, and you will make a sale. Focus on this, instead of the customer's current provider. John Wooden, the legendary former coach of the UCLA basketball team was once asked how he prepared to face other teams in games. Mr. Wooden replied that he prepared his team for his own plan, not the other teams.' Sell from strength, not weakness, and you will always be prepared.

10. "If I could match or beat the competitors deal, would you do business?"
    First of all, you don't even know that price is the real issue. Secondly, you are solidifying the low-ball figure that they have given you. Third, you are out of options and have nowhere to go from here.

The Emotional and Psychological Path to a Sale

Let's get into the best part of profiling—asking questions that allow you to understand someone's buying motives. Traditional sales training often discusses the process or steps to the sale, but neglects to consider the most important matter of all—what the buyer is thinking and feeling.

Here is an organizational and relationship chart for profiling:

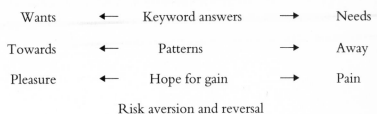

When you ask the right questions, customers will provide keyword answers that get to the heart of what will motivate them to buy. The answer to, "Mr. Customer, other than money or budgets, what is the most important item to you?" will be a specific keyword. Most customers have one, two, or maybe three top keyword issues. Customers don't tend to buy because of ten different things. Find out what is important and laser in on that. **Eliminate the Spray and Pray Method of Selling,** whereby you attempt to cover all bases instead of honing in on what is truly significant to a particular customer.

Keyword answers come in the form of wants and needs, and all decisions come from pleasure and pain motivators. People move towards the pleasure of what they want, and away from the pain of what they have. *Here's a tip.* . . People will move mountains for what they want, and they often won't go across the street for what they need. When customers talk about what they are "looking for," they are *want* buyers. They are seeking pleasure, and they don't have to buy; they just want to. When they discuss what they currently have and the pain that this particular object/action is causing, it's too big, too small, too slow, too fast, or their vendor isn't doing a good enough job, then they *need* buyers who are looking to move away from the pain. A need buyer almost walks backwards into a sale. They want to buy differently; so give them what they desire and sell them in a way that they want to buy. This process becomes less about selling and more about positioning them to buy.

Positioning the customer entails asking questions that pertain to his present or past situations for the product or service, such as the following:

1. "What do you like most about your current/past _____?"
2. "Is there anything you dislike about your current/past _____?"
3. "Think back to when you bought your current product/service. What was the first thing that made choose that product/service?"
4. "What are your current payments or budgets?"
5. "What cash investments/down payments did you make on your last purchase?"
6. "How much was your present/past product or service when you purchased it?"
7. "Has anything changed since you purchased your last product/service?"

Since people tend to adhere to the Law of Familiarity, patterns of behavior are to key to unlocking the future. Keeping your customers in comfortable behavior patterns reduces buying anxiety. In the automobile business, I often referred to the customer's trade-in as the "window to their buying soul." Usually, if you want a peek at someone's future, just look to his past. Try analyzing the customer's current or past product/service first. Take the example of a customer who walks into an automobile dealership to buy a vehicle. Most salespeople will ask the customer what he or she is looking for, and then immediately take the customer out to show them that type of vehicle. This process usually sets in motion the probability of low success and low profits—even if the sale is made.

Consider the following: What do you, as the salesperson, really know about the customer from the beginning of the buying process? Do you know the customer's key buying motives? Do you know the customer's wants or needs? Do you know the customer's buying patterns or buying personality? Do you know the buying cues that the customer's body language is giving?

When you immediately begin to sell a customer a product/service without knowing these answers, then you are a common peddler. You are spewing out information and hoping that it will match what the customer is looking to get. You are shooting a shotgun, when a rifle would work much better. When you don't have the information you need before you begin to present to the customer, you are showing a lack of concern and professionalism. You are merely wasting your time and displaying rank amateurism.

However, this is something that salespeople do far too often, usually for one of many different reasons. The first is simply that the salesperson does not know any better—they haven't been taught or haven't learned any differently. The second reason is that the salesperson does not believe in the importance of his or her job, and thinks that the product or service is mainly what sells the customer. And the third reason is the salesperson is merely lazy, and is skipping steps in the process.

Salespeople are often looking for the quick sale; but minimal effort usually leads to minimal results. When you take the time in the beginning of your interaction to educate yourself about the customer, you can create a laser-like sales presentation and demonstration. The irony of using the right approach is that spending a little more time in the beginning actually saves you more time in the long run.

Once you've gathered as much information as possible, you can apply my principal of **HFG—Hope for Gain.** The old television series *The Jeffersons* had a theme song entitled "Movin' On Up." When the Jeffersons became successful business people, they wanted to "move on up," which was not surprising to the show's viewers—after all, it's human nature to want to improve your situation. I have never had a customer tell me, "Mark, I want you to take me out of my product/service, put me into a worse product/service with worse features and benefits, and raise my price/payments." This just does not happen. Everyone is looking for **HFG—Hope for Gain.** *Here is a Big Idea:* Make sure you know what **HFG—Hope for Gain** looks like to your customer, and give them that.

As you gain knowledge of your customer, you will begin to understand their fears. Fear is the number one reason why your customer does not buy. The customer is generally afraid of making a mistake, usually in regards to the **3Ms—Money, Me, or Machine** (product/service).

To ease the sales process, and create the slippy-slide effect that I introduced in Chapter 9, you can practice **Risk Aversion.** Take the most common fears customers have, and put them into a positive light—in other words, erase the fear before it grows into a big hairy monster. Many customers, for example, have a fear of being pushed into a situation that they're not quite sure about. To practice Risk Aversion, simply tell the customer that you want to provide all of the information necessary for them to make a good decision—"whether that's today, or a month from now." Another technique to proactively reduce buying pressure is to ask the customer from the outset, "You don't have to buy today, do you?" When the stunned customer replies no, say, "It's okay if you do; but if not, I can check on a few things for the future as well."

The second way to address your customer's fears is to reverse them. Ideally, you want to practice Risk Aversion first to eliminate or soften the risk. But since the fear occasionally takes hold of a customer, this may force you to try to practice **Risk Reversal.** I will cover many approaches pertaining to this method in more detail later in the book; but for now, let me give you as an example one that I call the **"Lost Keys Close."** Let's say you have a customer who is shopping for a vehicle, and has found what she wants. She's excited about buying, but has some purchase anxiety. You would take the customer back to the vehicle that she was looking at, pull out a set of car keys, and ask her, "Have you ever started to get into your vehicle, and realized you don't have the car keys?" When the customer says yes, you continue. "When you realized you did not have the keys, you went back into the house and searched frantically. And after a long and frustrating hour you found them." Then ask the following, "Mrs. Customer, let me ask you a question. After you found your keys, how long did you keep looking? Obviously, you stopped. The reason that I am asking this silly question is, based upon what you had initially told me you were looking to buy and to accomplish—you have found it. Just like the keys, you don't have to keep looking. I will start the paperwork for you, and let you start enjoying your new vehicle as soon as possible." Even though I used an automobile purchase as an example, you can obviously use this same Risk Aversion technique creatively for any product or service.

Just as concerts can be better at different venues; sporting events can be more exciting in some arenas than in others; and parties can be more fun with certain themes—selling can be more effective if you set the stage. Even though the sale is about the customer, you create the show. Make sure it's one that they enjoy sitting through from beginning to end.

11

The Johnny Carson Principle

Questions as a Conversation

If you are old enough, you probably watched former late night talk show king, Johnny Carson. I have heard many people in the field talk about how easy Carson made his job look, despite how difficult the job really was. Several entertainers who were interviewed about Carson remarked that it could be extremely nerve-racking to be a guest on a talk show, but that Johnny Carson made them feel at ease. Many made the comment that Mr. Carson had a way of making so called "interviews" effortless, and that his questions seemed to be simply a normal part of conversation.

You must adopt this "Carson-esque" method to your sales dealings, and ask potential customers questions using a similarly conversational tone. Customers can't feel like they are being interrogated. You avoid setting this kind of a tone by asking questions and truly listening to the response; and then adding on to the answers, commenting, or asking them to clarify or expand upon what they've told you so far. You must be able to hear and understand your customers to truly be able to assist them. There is ample research that's proven that when people are listening to others, they are usually considering and forming their response while the person is still talking. You cannot sincerely pay attention to the customer when this occurs.

Traditional sales techniques, such as nodding your head up and down as your customer speaks, are potentially powerfully mirror imaging behaviors. However, if you focusing on nodding your head up and down mechanically in a less than genuine manner instead of concentrating on what the customer is trying to tell you, these techniques hurt more than they help. The point to remember here is really simple: be a person first, and a salesperson second.

Try using the following to help you not only listen to the customer, but to actively show the customer you are listening. Here is a great method I learned from Anne Baber (*Great Connections,* Impact Publishers, 1992).

Encourage
Acknowledge
Respond/**R**epeat

How can you use this? Try the following: *Encourage* your customer to talk to you by asking open-ended questions, which will allow him to expand on his original thoughts. Open-ended questions are the opposite of closed-ended questions, which simply elicit yes or no answers. Yes or no answers create choppy and interrogative type communications, and build potential objections and roadblocks to your sales process. In contract, an open-ended question would incite the customer to go into more detail and speak more freely. An example of this type of query would be, "What do you like most about this product or service?"

Simply asking such questions will stimulate dialogue, because a customer will spend 80 percent of the conversation answering the questions and adding on to their responses. When people talk, they feel important. You should make them feel more important, and always keep customers just above you; and you can do this by a process that I call "Adding through Subtraction." You add to a customer's intelligence, decision making, experience, or stature by subtracting from yours. You must humanize yourself. For example, a good professional speaker will show human frailties early and often during his speech. He wants to connect with his audience, and he does so by trying to make them feel like he is just like them, and makes the same dumb mistakes. When speakers humble themselves, their audience tends to become more receptive to their expertise and experience. They open themselves up to the speaker and allow them in. A good salesperson does this same thing.

Don't be afraid to apologize for small things. Doing so shows that you are human and humble. It shows potential clients that you are a person, and not a typical salesperson. Your choice of language is crucial to clearing the path for a sale and creating the slippy-slide effect we have discussed.

Positive Words and Phrases

Here are positive expressions of acknowledgment that I call **Tags**:

1. "I understand. . ."
2. "I appreciate that. . ."
3. "Sure!"
4. "You bet!"
5. "I propose" or, "You and I could propose"
6. "Fair enough?"
7. "I invite you to. . ."
8. "With your permission. . ."
9. "Would you allow me to. . ."

The above words and phrases acknowledge the customers, and let them know that you hear them. Even more importantly, the phrases are positive in nature. Former United States President, Bill Clinton said that to win the presidential election, a candidate had to be the most optimistic candidate and be able to convince the voters of that. Salespeople must similarly convince customers of their optimism, and these words and phrases help to convey this kind of positive spirit. Customers will not buy from a negative whining person. Let's look at a few examples of how to use this phrasing effectively.

Take a look at number 5—"I propose . . ." Instead of using the tired and negative sales phrase, "If I could . . . would you . . .?" Try using the phrase "I propose" or, "You and I could propose" instead. When you ask a customer, "If I could . . . would you . . .?" as a closing question in regards to price or terms, you scare the customer and often cause him to feel manipulated. This phrase makes you look like a creepy salesperson from a bad movie. I have actually had customers reply back, "Tell me if you can, and I will tell you if I will." If you were to say instead, "Mr. Customer, you and I could propose the following . . ." The phrase, "You and I could propose" does not have a negative connotation; and now you and the customer are on the same team.

Now let's look at number 6—"Fair enough?" I use this with customers repeatedly. When you use this phrase, you will find people will answer yes 100 percent of the time. Nobody wants to be unfair. We are raised to be fair and to share. When you suggest something and then follow it with the phrase "Fair enough?" you will build a positive momentum of agreement that eliminates any kind of manipulation.

When I first got married, I made a lot of communication mistakes with my wife, Kim. I used expressions such as "You need to," and, "You should." Women who are reading this can attest to the fact that this did not work well. Then I had a great idea. I could use sales approaches. Sales approaches work for everything!

I started to say things like, "Kim, I was just thinking about X. I thought you might be interested in this. I invite you to consider it." The difference in her response was amazing. I was getting almost everything I wanted. I almost felt guilty. Well, not quite; but almost. Then one day, I made a mistake. My wife attended one of my seminars and worked in the back of the room. At lunchtime my wife came up to me and said, "I invite you find a new phrase, buddy—fair enough?" So much for using sales techniques with your spouse.

The Real Questions

Now that we have addressed the questions that you must ask the customer, let's attend to the underlying questions that your customers are asking themselves about you and your product and service.

Question #1 – *Who are you, and why are you the best choice?*

Consciously or subconsciously, the customer is sizing up your every word and every move. You are like a jigsaw puzzle that they are putting together, piece by piece. You must be able to give them your **SDP—Specific Defining Proposition, or USP—Unique Selling Proposition.**

In other words, you must be able to tell a customer, in clear, concise language, why you are the unique and better choice. For years, traditional sales trainers have droned on and on about the power of giving features and benefits to the customer. Although giving features and benefits is great, in today's market, if that's all you do—you won't sell squat. You must have a strong positioning statement that contains a WOW factor; and you must be able to give strong evidence of its truth.

Take a moment right now and write down all the reasons why you think that your product is a unique and better choice. Now do the same thing for your business and yourself—that's right, even *you*. What makes you the better choice of a salesperson? Never, ever forget you. You will be the key.

Zig Ziglar has a great line: "Timid salespeople raise skinny kids." You cannot be timid in selling all of your unique and superior advantages. Most cultures teach us to be humble, a lesson that becomes hardwired into our brains. It gets distorted into a message that can hinder success. Remember the old saying: "It's not bragging, if it's true." Now, I am not telling you to attack your customer with an attitude that's all you, all the time; after all, I already discussed the importance of humbling yourself to your customers. However, you cannot go too far in either direction—you must be able to position yourself strongly in a manner that benefits your customer. Remember the radio channel, WIIFM—What's In It for Me? Your customer must hear and feel the confidence in your positioning.

The best way to appear confident and completely communicate your advantages is through a story. Remember: *Facts Tell, Stories Sell.* Customers process images and stories more easily than hard facts. They will identify with the story, and put themselves into the leading role. Facts make your claims seem like vague concepts; stories make them real. It's one thing to tell your customer you have the best product/service, or that you and your business are the best; it's totally different when you tell them specifically what makes you the best. This way, you can give them evidence and details in a story that demonstrates the truth and benefits of your claims, and shows them that you have a solution to their problem.

Let's go over the steps to answering the first question that customers are asking themselves about you—Who are you, and why are you the best choice?

- Make a point
- Tell a story with that point
- Recap the benefit of the story

Now, how do you get the most out of your storytelling? Consider your options. Which of the following kinds of stories might you tell?

- Similar situation stories
- Future-based stories
- Testimonials

Let's look at each one of these in detail.

Similar Situation Stories – Tell the customer a story based upon your own experience—or better yet, that of a customer—that demonstrates similar situations in regards to buying, making decisions, usage, and how they fared. Your customer needs *social proof;* he wants to know that he can be confident in his decisions. When customers hear that others made a great decision and are happy with it, they feel better. People tend to follow groups and adopt a herd mentality to rid themselves of the fear of being wrong, or embarrassed. A similar situation story is also known as the "feel, felt, found method." "Mr. Customer, I know how you *feel,* I have *felt* the same way, and what I *found* was . . ." This way, your customer sees not only that you went through the same thing; but also that you emerged success-fully, and that he can learn from your experience.

Future-Based Stories – Take the customer for a ride into the future. There isn't pressure in the future. If the customers can see it in their minds, they begin to feel it, and enjoy the emotions that the purchase might bring. This will logically validate their feelings. For example: "Mr. Customer, let's say that it's two weeks from now, and you have made a decision to buy. You have just signed the order, and the weight of making the decision is over. What is one thing that you can see that's allowing you to buy at that time?" When you get his answer, you may be able to learn about the one factor that will allow the customer to do business. The only difference between two weeks from now and today is the calendar.

Testimonial Stories – Remember the saying, *"If someone else toots your horn, it will be heard twice as far and twice as long as if you toot your own"*? Nothing is quite as strong as a direct testimonial. I have always kept a long list of customers who will give me a heartfelt, glowing, and specific per-sonal story without notice. You should have and use these testimonials in as many forms as possible, such as audio and video clips and letters. Put these stories on your web site, and have them in a portable form that is readily accessible. Keep what I call "brag books" with letters where cus-tomers speak of their wonderful experiences with your company. Keep CD's and DVD's of testimonials available to use at any time It's incredibly powerful when you can provide a long list of happy customers to a poten-tial client and tell them to call any and all of them at that moment.

The more specific the testimonial, the better it is. A generic comment like, "he/she is a great person," is worthless. People are, by nature, envious creatures, and they want the results that they see or hear that others have had. If I had to pick one area in which many salespeople and businesses fail to do a good enough job, it would be the use of testimonials. Because people have emotions, testimonials are an incredibly powerful source for salespeople.

Here's a shocking idea: Collect a few testimonials of customers who weren't exactly thrilled with you, your product, and service. Don't be afraid to share these with your customers as well—and here are the reasons why:

- **Honesty** – Your potential customer will immediately perceive you as honest, because you were willing to show your warts. Share with the client how this was an example of where you or your company had flaws that you learned to improve upon.
- **Believability** – Nobody—and I repeat *nobody*—has 100 percent customer satisfaction. If nobody has been unhappy with you, then you haven't done business. No matter how hard you try, you aren't going to please everyone. This may or may not be your fault—it does not matter. It's human nature to make mistakes, and your customers like to see both sides of the picture. They like it when you tell them of the rare occurrence where you screwed up and how you handled it. To show your mistakes makes your great testimonials more believable.
- **Uniqueness** – I can almost guarantee that you will be the only one in your field to display this kind of truthfulness. You will be unique. Embrace the fact that you, your product, and business are outstanding; but also embrace that you are human and that no product or business is infallible.

There are three stages that a customer goes through while buying. It is important to have the potential purchaser experience all three to successfully complete a sales process. They are:

1. Character
2. Emotion
3. Logic

Most of the time, buyers will move through the above three stages sequentially. From their very first contact with you, customers begin to form an impression and perceive your character and their ability to trust you. People want to trust who they buy from.

A first impression can involve several things, some of which can occur before a customer even meets you—such as your web site, the way that you or your receptionist answers the phone, the condition of the facility at which you work, the merchandising and display of your products or services, your emails, and more. Upon meeting you, potential buyers immediately form opinions about your initial greeting, your dress, your grooming, your demeanor, and your body language. They are developing impressions that answer the question "Can I trust you, your business, and product/service?"

Once this trust begins to take hold, the customer can move into the emotional phase of the purchase. No matter what anyone may say to the contrary, emotions play a hugely—if not the most—influential part of the sales process. Emotions that pertain to the purchase greatly influence decisions and outcomes. Recent discoveries of the brain have shown that previous thoughts about the sequence of behavior were incorrect. Older teachings on the functionality of the brain stated that thought preceded emotion; however, new discoveries now show that emotions come first, and help to create and cultivate thoughts. Using this newfound information in regards to the above sequence tells us that the customer's emotions help to create his thoughts and perceptions of your character.

People have to feel good about you, the product, the service, and the business—so all the logical reasons to buy can go right out the window without the appropriate emotions. Everyday, people buy products and services that aren't the best for them, or that they can't afford, usually for emotional reasons. But your job is not to play the role of good decision cop. Customers are entitled to make their own decisions, whether they make sense or not. Every day, people buy clothes, cars, houses and boat loads of services they cannot afford. We are a society of consumerism. Don't fight it—use it. If you do not feel morally comfortable with this idea, you must either find a product or service you feel this does not apply to; or get out of sales. Period, end of story. Unless you are a sociopath, you will not be successful going against your own moral compass.

Logic combines with and justifies emotion in the purchase. You must give logical evidence to justify the customer's decision to take action on his desires. People know their emotions are leading them, but they want to be able to say logically why it's okay to make a particular purchase. Logic can come in the form of the usage of the product or service, the poor performance of the previous product or service, or even money.

People justify buying a lot more than they need, because they can afford to make the payments or credit card payments. It does not matter if the term is 72 or 84 months on a finance contract, or a 40-year mortgage, or that the reason they are going to finance this purchase is because they don't have the money. The real reason that they are making a purchase is that people buy emotionally and justify logically. Give lots of logical reasons to support the emotional decision. Try the following for both emotional and logical reasons.

Tewart's 4 P'S of the Customer's Buying Decisions

- **Performance** – Customers will pay for performance. I personally bought a Kubota tractor with zero turn radius, 28 horsepower, diesel engine, and a 60-inch deck to mow my acreage. It was not the cheapest tractor I could have bought; I bought the tractor because it cut my mowing time in half. And okay, I also bought it because it's fast as hell and actually makes mowing fun. So sue me! I bought it when I already had a perfectly good tractor because the performance would save me, my wife, or whoever mowed our lawn two hours of their time. Personally, I will pay large sums of money to create spaces of usable time that I never had before. Time is the most valuable currency to me, and probably to many of your customers—who will pay substantially for it.

- **Pride of Ownership** – Most buying decisions that are made for products or services—even those in a corporate environment—are due to Pride of Ownership, otherwise known as ego. Several Lexus vehicles are nothing more than a Toyota made more prettily, and with a much bigger price tag. Customers buy the Lexus vehicle in droves when they could have had the Toyota and saved a bunch of money, because of ego. Every company and every person buys something because of this reason—nobody is immune. The next time one of your customers is wavering because their logic tells them their ego is out of control, just tell them it is okay, because they deserve it. "Sir, you work hard, and you deserve it." If you are a salesperson that sells to large corporations, just remember that these entities are made up of individual people with their own logic, emotions, and egos. Always sell to people, not to corporations.

- **Protection –** Many customers desire protection, which can come in the form of safety, or safety in decision. If I were to ask my wife what is the most important thing to her when she buys a vehicle, she would answer, safety. For her safety would trump performance, pride of ownership, or even a good deal. It's her dominate buying motive and keyword. If a salesperson is to sell her a product or service it would be wise to mention the words safe, safer, safety, and safely as much as possible.

My wife and I once went to look at a Lexus vehicle, and the salesperson we dealt with did several smart things. First, he asked who the primary driver would be, and then if there would be any secondary drivers? This question established the buyer as my wife, and made it clear that I would be involved as a secondary party. Many salespeople would have incorrectly just sold to me as the male, and lost the sale to my wife—while also being offensive. Next, the salesperson asked my wife what the most important thing to her was when purchasing a vehicle. As I turned to my wife to watch and listen for her answer, she answered "safety," without thinking or blinking. The salesperson then built his entire presentation and demonstration by weaving the theme of safety into it.

The salesperson said the words safe, safer, safely, safety, and safest so many times I thought my wife's head would spin off her shoulders. By the end of the presentation, my wife was like one of Pavlov's dogs—almost foaming at the mouth when she got out of the car and said to me, "This is the safest car I have ever seen!"

The salesperson had performed sales art and science all at once. He had a sale for the taking. But as many salespeople erroneously do every day all over the world, he never assumed the sale, or asked for the order. He assumed, incorrectly, he could not sell the car that day; and he never gave us a chance to buy. He even gave us the dismissal slip—the dreaded brochure, and a request for us to come back and see him when we were ready. He lacked what I call, *"Sales Esteem."* Lesson relearned: **TLC—Think Like a Customer.**

- **Profit** – The last P is for profit, by which I mean a value or monetary consideration. If someone shops a product or service—if that person considers all other things equal—then the customer will buy on the profit or price motivation. There are some customers who give the price or profit motive far more weight than others. This type of customer will buy just about anything because it has the lowest price. Price trumps quality or value in his mind. Fortunately for you, that type of customer is a lot rarer than you might believe. Few people are driven only by price. Weak and underperforming salespeople tend to use price as a major customer objection a lot more than it really exists. The price objection becomes an excuse for underperforming salespeople.

The 4 Ps work, no matter what type of product or service the customer is buying. All products or services have a performance value, pride of ownership, and ego qualities. All products or services have a protection or safety element, and all products and services have profit, value, or money considerations.

I remember John Wayne saying in one of his movies, "Mister, you're just spitting out words to see where they land." That phrase reminds me of a common fatal flaw of most salespeople; talking without a direction. Don't just talk. Don't just ask questions. Have conversations. Listen and utilize what you learn. Communication is a two-way process. Being a sales superstar takes the skills of a very great communicator.

12

I'll Take Door Number Two— Selection Time

We had a saying in the automobile business: "There's an ass for every seat." This simply means that people are different, and they have wide varieties of tastes. Something that you may think is ugly or does not make sense might be beautiful and make perfect sense to someone else.

My family and I attend a Unity Church in Cincinnati. One Sunday, we were given a sermon by a visiting preacher named Damon Lynch. Reverend Lynch had gained a lot of notoriety during and after the Over-The-Rhine Riots in Cincinnati in 2001. He had become a spokesperson for large segments of the African American community in the inner city of Cincinnati.

Lynch is an understandably controversial figure, and many segments of the city's population consider his messages divisive. However, his sermon that Sunday morning struck a chord with me in many ways. Reverend Lynch discussed the same concept that we touched on with our oft-used industry phrase—how different people can see the same things in many different ways, based upon their life experiences or culture. Everyone has his or her own kaleidoscope.

This message led me to think of customers and their kaleidoscopes as well. You must listen, step back, and—as Claude Hopkins said in his book *My Life in Advertising and Scientific Advertising* (McGraw Hill, 1966)—"You must enter into the conversation already going on in the customers head." So much of selling is actually allowing the customer to buy. I often say that "To be successful, you often have to get out of your own way." The late great blues guitarist Luther Allison said, "Leave your ego, play the music, and love the people." I think Mr. Allison's saying works for just about anything—including sales. As a salesperson, you have to keep your ego from blocking the customer making a choice. You have to play your music; which in your case is the art and science of sales. You have to love the people to want to help them.

In my career, I have heard every imaginable negative and nasty saying used to describe a customer. Rats, mooches, lay-downs, grinders, gear heads, flakes—just to name a few. I am even sad to admit that I have been as guilty as any salesperson of using some of those terms. It's hard to consider the customer first when you are coming from such a negative and adversarial position. Hopefully, when you sell, someone buys. These two things are mutually inclusive. Selling so that someone can buy is something you do *with* your customer, not *to* them.

Assisting your customer in the selection of the product/service is a big part of that process. Remember these two phrases: "Investigate before you demonstrate," and "Negotiation without investigation and demonstration leads to frustration." Short-cuts in the selling process are a quick path to bad results. After you have done your homework and listened to your customer, you can offer direction and assistance, and even guide the customer in an educated fashion. You will avoid the "Spray and Pray" method of selling, wherein a salesperson begins to immediately talk about the product or service without trying to figure out what the customer's wants, needs, or problems are.

Remember that perception is everything. If a person calls a real estate agent to see a certain house, that agent should make sure to select a couple of other houses to offer choices to the customer. Try the "Power of Three." For whatever reason, the world seems to resonate with the number three—the Three Musketeers, the Three Stooges, the Three Wise Men—tap into this magical number yourself. When you only show one option, customers perceive this as *take it or leave it*. When you give two options, it's perceived as, *either or*. For whatever reason, three seems to be the perfect number to choose from, because three seems to offer a real choice. More than three, however, leads to confusion. Have you ever looked at houses with real estate agents and saw so many at once that you couldn't remember which was which—and they all seemed to run together? Can you pick out the one central theme with this particular experience that led you to become so confused? Those real estate agents did not do their homework to discover the right choices. They sold by trial and error. Often, salespeople like this leave you tired, perplexed, and irritated by your lack of progress.

A customer calls a real estate agent, and wants to look at a property. The agent pants like a dog and agrees to meet the customer to hopefully get a bone. The agent usually spends a ton of time, effort, and headache, yet he usually gets low results for his troubles. Let me ask you this question: "In this instance, what did the salesperson know about the customer?" The answer is nothing. Therefore, how could the salesperson assist the customer in the selection?

If you had a framework of your customers' emotional and psychological markers—as we discussed earlier—you could choose two other houses to wrap around the house they called about. You can choose a house lower in value and one higher in value to frame the choice. Educated customers love choice, because it acknowledges and substantiates the research they have done for this purchase. Give them this choice. Uneducated customers love choice as well, because it allows them to feel appreciated and empowered. Give your customers well thought-out and smart choices. I have had real estate agents take me to many houses that they had never seen before—and they had no idea or thought about the emotional and psychological framework of my potential buying decision.

When you give alternatives to your customer, you accomplish several of the following things:

- Test commitment
- Satisfy shopping needs
- Enhance proper selection
- Allow the customer to "save face" financially
- Establish response for possible negatives in negotiations
- Increase urgency
- Allow clear choices
- Move away from price-only decisions
- Physically involve buyer
- Emotionally involve buyer
- Show a caring attitude on your part
- Differentiates you from other salespeople

Setting the Environment

You should build the proper environment for the selection of the product or service. When doing so, try to avoid the following mistakes made by salespeople in various fields:

- Auto salespeople who are willing to show a dirty vehicle.
- Real estate salespeople who show a cluttered house.
- Home improvement salespeople who don't show before and after pictures of completed projects, and who neglect to bring physical specimens of materials.
- Water treatment salespeople who can't show the difference their product can make because they did not bring a test kit.

Many times, in automotive sales seminars, I have had salespeople argue that they can't show a clean car at their location. My reply is always, "BS." Imagine the following scenario:

As you approach a vehicle with a potential customer, you say to him, "Please wait a second Mr. Customer. I apologize, but this vehicle is dirtier than I would like. We try hard to keep the cars clean, but road construction is making it difficult. However, I refuse to show you a vehicle that you are considering spending a lot of hard-earned dollars for that is this dirty. I really am sorry, but I am going to take this to the back really quickly and spray and wipe it off so you can get a good look at it—fair enough?" You have now created reciprocity. The customer has seen your extra effort and carefulness, and he begins to feel a sense of obligation. In other words— you are earning the trust and commitment of the customer through your diligence in setting the appropriate environment.

If you are in real estate sales, don't show a house that is too hot or too cold. Get to the site early and make sure it feels right, looks right, and smells right. If you are selling a vehicle, make sure it's not too hot or cold, and that the customer can get a sense of the "new car" smell. If you are a CPA meeting a new client, clear the clutter from your desk and office. All of these things are fairly small efforts that will have a big impact on your customer's perception of the product.

All too often, I hear salespeople say that these things aren't always possible to do. Why not? Quit whining and allowing crappy results, and do what others won't do. End of story. One powerful first impression is more valuable than a bunch of average or bad showings.

I once knew a Toyota salesperson that would drive his clients to the top of a canyon and park the vehicle. He would ask the customer to get out of the vehicle and step back from it to take a look at the beautiful view of the canyon in the background. He would smile and remark how that scene made the vehicle looked like a picture postcard, and he told them that it would look just as good in their garage. All of this may sound like syrupy sales talk to you; but the customers loved the visualization. This salesperson sold a ton of vehicles, because he understood how important it was to set the environment right from the beginning.

Showtime

Earlier in this book, I said that it was Showtime from the minute you greet your customer. P. T. Barnum has often been misquoted as saying, "There is a sucker born every minute." What he really said was, "There is a customer born every minute." Barnum was a master marketer and salesperson, and he gave his customers an incredible show. Never forget that every minute of your sales cycle is Showtime—and never forget that a major part of the show is making your presentation and demonstration.

Whether you sell a product or service, you have to make a strong presentation and demonstration to get the emotional buy in required to make a sale. Whether you are in advertising and making a presentation for an account, or you are selling vacuum cleaners, you must give the customer something that makes them say "WOW."

As it was when P.T. Barnum coined the above phrase, selling is still part circus. No matter what customers say, they want to be entertained when they buy. For years, companies have been bringing together focus groups to listen to what customers say they want to have or experience. The problem is that what people say they want in focus groups and what they *really* want are often two different things. People will give social speak answers or politically correct information in focus groups—so, unfortunately the bottom line is that most focus groups are worthless.

Here's an example of this "focus group" phenomenon: I once owned a vending machine company. When we placed the machines, we offered a menu of items to the decision maker, who was usually the office manager. The theory behind the menu was that it would create buy-in from the decision maker. It was my personal observation that in many cases, the office managers struggled with issues that revolved around their workers' weight. A majority of time, the office manager would choose a lot of healthy, low-calorie or low-carb snacks. After we had serviced the machines several times we began to notice a trend. Every time—and I do mean every time—a person requested the healthier snacks, they didn't sell, and we would have to throw them away.

What people say they will do and what they really do often vary drastically. You must have a presentation and demonstration that will satisfy what someone *wants* to do, what they think they *can* do, and what they probably *will* do. Presenting and demonstrating products or services is a lot like playing pool: A bad pool player plays one shot a time. A good pool player shoots while planning a couple of shots ahead. A *great* pool player plays the whole game in his head on every shot. A great salesperson sells the same way.

Presenting any product or service requires you to think about where the presentation starts, where the middle will be, and where it will end—much like a book or a play. If you are presenting a vehicle, you may plan a 7-step walk-around presentation. Most trainers in the automotive industry teach their trainees to start a vehicle presentation in the front of the vehicle. However, in a quarter of century of selling, I have rarely seen a customer begin at the front of the vehicle. Notice I said customer. That's right; once again, it's about the customer. Most potential car buyers want to go immediately to the window sticker (if there is one) to look at pricing. Most sales approaches teach you to stay away from pricing. Good luck on that idea. The Contrarian Approach dictates that you take customers exactly where they want to go, so if it's the window sticker—then go there. If a salesperson wants to know where to start—just open every door, the hood, and the trunk, stand back and tell the customer enthusiastically, "Take a look." The customer will go wherever he or she wants to go—and that's where you begin. This theory holds true whether you sell a product or a service. Learn to address the *issue* of price up front; because when you do so, it tends to go away without you having to scare the customer or get into the topic of discounting your price.

For many years in the auto industry, manufacturers would hold national walk-around presentation competitions for salespeople. The dirty little secret that nobody wanted to talk about was that most of the winners were *not* the best sales performers. My argument was that the slick presentation was too generic. It was a one-size-fits-all show-and-tell. Customers want to relate to a person who asks and listens, but not a salesperson that shows and tells.

How can you address a customer's wants and needs and personalize potential solutions to the customer's problems unless you know what they are? This takes the tailored, laser beam approach that we discussed in earlier chapters, rather than a shotgun approach. Some of the best presentations made by any salesperson for any product or service look like a made-for-the-customer movie. On several episodes of Donald Trump's TV show, *The Apprentice,* I watched time after time while a highly-degreed supposed "sales superstar" started exhibiting products, ads, or services with absolutely zero knowledge of its customer, company, product, service, or core audience. On one episode a contestant bragged of his sales acumen—and then made the worst, most offensive presentation I have ever seen. No, it wasn't a bad day; he just didn't put his customer first. It was apparent that instead, his ego always came first. *BIG LESSON: It's always about the customer.*

Oftentimes in the auto industry, presentations begin and end inside the vehicle. It's always great to end where the customer can utilize the product or service for himself. If you are selling an ad or service, your presentation should end with the customer envisioning himself using or benefiting from the product ad or service. This is what I call allowing them to see the end result in their *mind's eye.* If you are selling a couch, you should have the customer sit on it, and then ask him to imagine where the couch would be in his home. Ask him to see himself watching TV while sitting on the couch, and ask him—"How does that feel?" and "Can you see this in the room?" If you are selling a tractor, they better use it first. If you are selling real estate, you had better paint the picture of the customer living there. Have the customer imagine the closer drive to his children's school, the grocery stores, and sitting on the back deck. If you are selling life insurance, they better see the grave and picture their family's well-being as if they were already in it.

A great product presentation and demonstration contains three elements we've already discussed—visual, auditory, and kinesthetic. Most salespeople talk a lot and make verbal presentations; but as noted in a previous chapter, the majority of people process information in a visually dominate manner. So this manner of presenting is kind of like talking loud to a deaf person. When you demonstrate a product, don't be afraid to really engage the customer in the dominant aspects of the product or service. Earlier in the book I talked about my wife Kim looking at and test driving a Lexus. Kim had mentioned that safety was her primary concern. The salesperson did not just take her for a regular test drive; he had her apply her anti-lock brakes at a high rate of speed. He had Kim put on the gas going around a pretty steep curve. The experience of the vehicle was awesome; you can't put those feelings into words.

Several years later, my wife bought a Land Rover. The test drive tracks at Land Rover dealerships take the vehicle through an off road experience that will blow your mind. The vehicle is put on a track that requires it to virtually lean up and down. When you go on that test drive, you are comfortable that your vehicle won't tip over, and you truly feel that you will be safe in that vehicle. Once again, your presentation demonstration must contain the WOW aspect of "Showtime."

Always assume that your customers want a demonstration; don't ask. Customers aren't looking for a loaf of bread when they are looking for your product or service. If you ask a potential client, he will often reply "no" out of reluctance to make such a decision—and then you have lost the sale. In this case, live by the Nike slogan: "Just Do It."

My family experienced this "WOW" moment as customers when we shopped for a hot tub. The salesperson showed us the features and benefits of the tub, and he told us about his own hot tub—but he didn't leave it at that. He took us into a back room and showed us a model filled with water that was similar to the one we were considering. He told us that this was the hot tub that we were going to try out. He didn't ask; he told us, and assumed that we would want to try it out, in a positive way. He instructed us to go home and get our bathing suits on—and come back to test the hot tub in a private and secure area. Although we told him this wasn't necessary, he said he wouldn't feel right unless we did. He wanted us to be 100 percent sure of our decision. Later on, my son, wife, and I were in the hot tub, trying out the different jets, the radio, the waterfall, the lights, and anything else we could play with. We had a blast, and we bought the hot tub. If a salesperson can successfully assume the demonstration of a hot tub, then there is no excuse not to demonstrate what you sell.

Here's another tip: Let your customer end the demonstration. The demonstration is the most peak emotional time. Let the customer savor it.

At the end of your demonstration, your customer is combining emotion and logic at a rapid rate. This is where the logic justifies the emotional decision. You will get questions about price, payments, warranty's guarantees, service, rates, terms, delivery, and other customers and their experiences. Don't be afraid of these questions; they should be music to your ears. This means your customer is ready and willing to buy your product or service.

For those of you who sell products or services that you think may not lend themselves to active and involved presentations, I invite you to open your mind and get creative. Can you create a video of the product in use? Can you create a video of the product to show what it looks like in its environment? If you sell an intangible product, can you create a video around potential scenarios of how the product or service might be used— and also include the testimonials that were mentioned earlier? Simple technology would allow you to create these kinds of media, and have them on your web site or on www.youtube.com in no time. Go over the sizzle of the benefits in a way that customers can truly experience.

Five Keys to Peak Performance

When you present and demonstrate your product or service, you must become aware of five factors within you. All success starts in and works outward.

1. Energy/Enthusiasm
2. Emotion
3. Empathy
4. Humor
5. Message

One night, while I was on a trip promoting my seminars, I received a call from one of our company's sales representative who was selling for me in a different city. We were going over our results for the day, week, and month. The salesperson in the other city was working hard, but was not getting anywhere near the results that we were getting. We were diligently breaking down all of his actions to try to figure out why.

After that phone call, I spent the rest of the evening trying to come up with the answer to his question. But in doing so, I stumbled upon the answer to a much bigger question: "Why do some people succeed, when others fail?" Working harder is the answer most people give; however, I realized that is often not the only answer—and in many instances, it is not the correct answer. After all, this rep was working just as hard as we were. However, when I had the salesperson role-play his day back to me word-for-word and step-by-step, critical elements were missing from the hard work. He lacked energy and enthusiasm, and *Showtime* had left his body. One no led to another no, and that led to a "no" demeanor. The word enthusiasm is derived from the Greek 'breath of God,' and it's a contagious state of being. Vince Lombardi said it best: "If you aren't fired with enthusiasm, you will be fired with enthusiasm." This particular employee of mine had lost his emotional approach to the customer. When you sell with emotion, you automatically use voice tone, voice inflection, and body language to convey conviction and sincerity. Emotion is, and always will be, the number one factor that sells. Feelings can move mountains, make no mistake about it. You can't fake emotion, either. But as great actors channel the emotions of their characters so strongly that you believe they *are* that character; so can you channel your emotions to be you.

As we know, most movies, TV, theater, and other media portray salespeople as self-centered sharks. But any sales superstar who enjoys lasting results is the polar opposite of that persona. Studies of sales superstars continually show strong empathy as one of the key components to their success. By now, you are getting used to me beating the drum with my mantra so here we go again: You must TLC—Think Like a Customer.

Humor is another important part of this—and it makes everything in life easier. Laughter releases endorphins in your brain that make you feel good. People enjoy being around people who make them laugh. I have never seen a customer who was buying something, while laughing, tell the salesperson that they were buying from them because they didn't like or trust him. Show me a laughing customer, and I will show you a buying customer. Cavett Robert, the founder of the National Speakers Association was once asked if you had to use humor in your speeches. His reply was, "Only if you want to get paid."

I am not asking you to be a stand-up comedian as a salesperson; in fact, using humor too soon and too often in a sale is risky. Instead, consider how most comedians get their best material—the great ones simply find humor in the everyday occurrences of life.

Start a journal where you make notes of things you did and experiences you had for the day. Take some quiet time and think of the humor in these simple life experiences. Make note of humor in TV shows, plays, comedians, and in others around you. Your best material is your own life. When you begin to look for humor, you will find it, and you will strengthen your humor muscle. Use the humor in those experiences to relate to the customers' own life experiences. In many ways, we are all very similar, and when people smile and laugh, they usually buy.

The last component of this self-evaluation is your message. You must believe in what you are selling, and truly believe that it provides a solution. Even if the customer is a "want" buyer, that customer's desire should become so strong that it is now a problem that has to be solved. That's where your message that matches their problem comes in.

Here is the big kicker ... *The best message in the world won't matter if it is not seen, heard, or felt.* How do you make sure the message is received? By using the first four components—Energy/Enthusiasm, Emotion, Empathy, and Humor. Then, get the message delivered. Most salespeople make the critical mistake of spending all of their time on the message, and not on the delivery components. Follow these steps in the correct order, and watch your sale come to fruition.

It's Better to Ask Forgiveness Than to Ask for Permission

That saying may not apply to everything in life, but it does apply to the next part of your sales process—**The Assumptive Stage.** Don't ask people if they want to buy. Give them an opportunity to keep moving forward with the purchase. Here's the good news: If you did everything that this book has instructed so far, you often won't ever have to ask for the business— because the people will want to buy so badly that they will be taking your product or service without any extra effort on your part.

At the end of the sales process, most salespeople ask silly, traditional, trial closing questions like, "If I can get the price/terms/service right, can we do business today?" Anytime you hear yourself use the old, "If I could/ would you" close that I have warned you about before, just stick a needle in your face as a painful reminder to break yourself of this 1950s salesperson jargon. This old trial close frightens your customer, and often elicits a negative response. You may actually be scaring your potential buyer into saying, "No, not today. We have to think about it first." You have spent hours, weeks, months, or years getting your customer to the point of saying yes, and what do you do? You scare them and make them say no. Remember the slippy-slide. Don't insert a roadblock.

Assume the sale by asking non-threatening but assumptive questions.

"Other than money or terms, is there anything else that would keep you from owning/purchasing?"

"Is there anything you would like to add, change, or fix before we get your proposal?"

"What do you like best about your product or service?"

"Is there anything you don't like about your product or service?"

Assume the sale with assumptive statements such as:

"Do you want the ads to start immediately, or next week?"

"How will you be registering and titling your RV?"

"Who will be the beneficiary on this policy?"

"Will you be taking a mortgage for the property? If so, do you need lending institutions?"

"I will gas up the boat. Do you want it delivered, or will you be towing it with you?"

"Let's get a proposal and give it a try!"

"Where is the first vacation you are taking your boat/vehicle/RV to?"

Assumptive questions and statements do the following:

- Replace traditional trial close questions
- Ease the buying process
- Reduce negative responses
- Reduce customers fears
- Move the customer to the final stages

Present and demonstrate your product or service as if this is the *last customer you will ever have*. Your customers deserve to get a show; it doesn't have to be flashy and it doesn't have to have bells and whistles; but it should put you, your product or service, and your business in a superior position to win. The show should be heartfelt, and should display the human element of emotion. Every product or service deserves a good presentation—and your customers deserve to get one.

13

How to Get the Sale, Contract, and $

Once you have completed the presentation and demonstration of your product or service, you can move into the proposal stage. If you are selling a product or service where you have already presented figures, you should think about how you can reorder your sales process so that you are not giving the final figures up front. This is by no means impossible, despite what you may think. Many of you are selling to corporations that have RFPs (Requests for Proposal). I would recommend that you stop the typical salespeople "begging" that often occurs during this phase in the selling process. If all you do is send a proposal, your sale will probably be about price only. You must change the game.

Some salespeople will argue until they are bankrupt that they are selling a commodity, and they can't differentiate or change the game. Some salespeople will argue that their industry, area, or company is different.

The answer is simple: These salespeople are all dead wrong. You can *always* change something—here are some examples:

- Package
- Service
- Terms
- Guarantee
- Warranty
- Product
- Speed of delivery
- Availability
- Method of payment
- Appearance of the same product
- Bonuses

Change the game, or change your career. In the chapter on marketing, I discussed strategies for getting an appointment with a decision maker. You can use the same type of strategies to get in front of the decision maker before you give a proposal on a RFP. Separate yourself from the crowd. As a reminder, here are a few of the strategies I discussed, as well as some additional ideas.

- Send a FedEx package to the CEO or decision maker with a CD and a note that guarantees to add a certain number or dollar of sales in just two minutes by listening to the CD on their drive home. Record the CD and give one dynamic solution to a problem and mention that you will call on a certain date and time to give them two other solutions as well.
- Send a trash can mailer, brown bag mailer, photo development bag, or some other form of dimensional mail to the decision maker.
- Send a singing telegram.
- Google the company and officers and go to www.zoominfo.com to research their most current company information, which you can then use to tailor your contact attempts.
- Go to Google News Alerts and have the latest news information on this company emailed to you. Use these facts in your messages,

emails, or marketing pieces to get yourself in front of the decision maker before your proposal. Make them feel that you eat, breathe, and live their company.

■ Get a copy of the company's annual report and dig for material that you can use to get in front of the decision maker, and to adapt your proposal. Think in terms of the pleasure versus pain motivators that we covered earlier in the book.

■ Check Google for reports on CEO speeches or company meetings to find the important buzzwords, strategies, goals and the company's current pains and problems. Target your information, contact attempts, and proposals using this information. You will either get the customer to call you, take your call, get noticed, or elevate the value of your proposal. These strategies give you a way to move to the top of the heap.

Don't be like the majority of salespeople; don't over think the reasons why you can't do or consummate the sale. This is a point where self-defeating mechanisms run rampant in the sales game. There is a sales axiom that the masses tend to ignore, "You can't sell what you don't attempt." Don't find reasons not to give people the opportunity to buy.

I have heard a myriad of excuses from salespeople as to why they should not move forward with a customer. The trade-in wasn't there, the spouse wasn't there, the customer said that he won't buy today, they are going to go shop your figures, the company won't be in the market for three months, the customer had to think about it, there isn't enough money in the budget, the payments or terms are too high . . . I can't tell you how many dollars of goods and services I have sold by not listening to excuses. I don't believe in excuses. Not all customers will buy today; but I know they *can't* buy today if I don't professionally give them an opportunity to do so.

How to Handle Customer Questions and Comments
5 Step Process
1. Listen
2. Agree
3. Address

4. Segue (Bridge)

5. Redirect

When you are in the middle of a sales process, customers will naturally ask questions or make comments. You must be prepared to handle these *moments of truth* when they come up. I give them this name because an educated salesperson can easily handle and use these moments to gain the trust and confidence of the customer. If they miss the moment, they not only miss an opportunity; but they will usually blow the sale because of it. Handling customer questions is where the rubber meets the road in a sale.

It sounds trite to say you must listen to the customer, but I want you to think back to times when you were trying to communicate something to a salesperson, and that individual either wasn't listening—or was listening with an agenda. It's incredibly frustrating, and it makes you angry. You can probably recall many times that this has happened to you; now, think of them and imagine how the customer feels.

Try this listening technique: When a customer finishes with a comment or questions, count to three before responding. Give the customer the time to completely finish his train of thought. Use facial gestures to show that you are both listening to and considering what was said. Do not run over the customer's words.

Next, you should always agree with the customer. "I understand," "Sure," "You bet," "Absolutely," and "Interesting" are all phrases of acknowledgement. Never give the customer the right to fight you. It's easier to agree with the customer and merge their beliefs with yours later than it is to insist you are right from the start. Lose the battle to win the war. People like being right—it's human nature. Never ever fight human nature in sales. You will always lose.

Here is another area where my Contrarian Method of selling differs greatly from traditional sales training. In traditional methods you use *bypass* techniques which tell you to ignore the customer and move on. In the Contrarian Method, you address the customer's questions. You look the person right in the eye, answer positively, and have a plan of how to deal with any query or comment that might follow. There are times where you may only be addressing the issue of their question with the promise to answer more fully later on; but you *are* acknowledging the question and its importance to you. Traditional sales training tells salespeople to either ignore the question or statement unless it comes up at least three times, or to use the *bypass* technique. Earlier in the book, I briefly explained *bypass* techniques—but this concept bears repeating. Bypass techniques teach the salesperson to sidestep the question without addressing the issue in some manner, and to instead ask what I feel is an insulting question. For example, the customer may ask "What is your best price on this widget?" The bypass response to that question is, "When will you be using your new widget?" or, "Who is the lucky one who is getting this new widget?" You are avoiding the issue, and you are creating conflict.

I believe that using these techniques—or ignoring a customer's questions—leads to an angry customer. Angry customers often don't tell you they are mad; they just vote with their feet and their wallets. At this point of a lost sale, uneducated salespeople begin to blame the customer or make excuses.

There are ways that you can address an issue without necessarily spilling all the beans at the point of question; let me give you an example. A salesperson is showing a customer a new computer and the customer asks, "What is your best price on this computer?" You listen and realize that a customer can only ask so many things about your product or service. Price is just a natural question. However, you must realize that any price you quote at this time—no matter how low—does not create urgency for the customer to buy. In fact, no matter how low you quote the price, it will only create doubt in the customer's mind—is this the lowest or best price? You have, in effect, given your customer a permission slip to shop. You have taken a normal question of price and, by mishandling the question, you have given the issue of price super powers. Customers can say that they just want the lowest price; but it's positively, absolutely not the case. As we discussed before, hardly anyone buys on price alone. And if they do, you may not want them as customers anyway. The customers who you make little to no profit on are always the customers who complain the most and seem to eat up your time with constant problems. The customers from whom you make a better profit are the customers who send you gifts and bring you vegetables from their garden.

After you listen to a question about price, make sure to acknowledge the customer and address the question by saying something such as, "Absolutely, I will make sure to get you the best possible value on this computer. Just to let you know, every computer in this store will have a different sales value based upon how long it has been in inventory, the supply and demand of the particular type and model, and any sales or promotions we may have now or upcoming. In fact, just so I can get you the best value on this, let me ask me ask you a couple of questions that will help. Are you going to be looking only at a PC equipped as this one is, or might you be considering a model with either more or less features? Are you interested in looking at any pre-owned? Would you like to compare this computer to one that might have a few hours of usage, but a remaining warranty, and possibly substantial savings? Will you want to see figures with and without a trade-in? What kind of features does your current PC have?"

Address the issue with what I call a "word track"—which was my initial response to the question. I told the customer that I would answer his question, how I would answer his question, and what information I needed to answer his question properly; then I use the segue technique as demonstrated. Notice that after I used a word track to address the question, I then segued or bridged from there to redirecting the sales process by asking the customer questions. The phrase "by the way" acted as a bridge in this example. I also gave the customer a reason for my questions, which provided me with leverage to be able to redirect the flow of the sales process. I did this by telling the customer that his answers to the questions would help us to establish the best possible value or deal for him. Every step and every word was executed based upon the self-interest of the customer. You must acknowledge the customers' questions and desires up front. By recognizing the importance of their needs and then giving a benefit to the customer with my questions, I am avoiding an argument or conflict on his question.

Here is the amazing lesson: When you learn this, practice this, and then do this with confidence with your customer, you will find that over 95 percent of time, the issue of price does not come back up until you bring it up yourself. It's a fact that if price precedes value you either lose or you are an order taker for small profit.

Stop reading this book after this paragraph! I invite you to put this book down and grab a piece of paper to write down a top ten list of questions and comments that occur during your sales process that either tend to stump you or cause problems. Then I want you to write down how you are currently responding to those questions. Next, I want you to compare your current response to my five step formula and what you have learned. Lastly, I invite you to keep rewriting it until you believe you have improved and tightened your words and sequence as much as possible.

Here's my question for you: Will you really do the exercise? Or will you live like most salespeople—making excuses? If you think this exercise is hard, try digging a ditch. That's hard. Selling simply takes determination and persistence. Persistent = Consistent. If you are persistent in your education and approach, you will be consistent in being a sales superstar. Just do what others are not dedicated enough or too lazy to do.

Competence = Confidence. You can only become competent through repetition. Repetition is the mother of all skill. Here is some other great news for you: If you are the rare sales professional that actually takes the information from this book and studies it, practices it, and implements it, you will be so far ahead of your competition that things will become much easier. You will become so confident, that sales situations with a customer that used to scare you will no longer faze you at all. There is an old saying, "No part-time customer should outwit a full-time salesperson." Be prepared so you can fully help your customer.

Let's look at some ideas to address common objections and questions that arise during the sales process.

Common Questions

1. "What's Your Best Price?"

Use the 5-step process and the following word track

"All of our products/programs/services will have different values based upon availability, time in inventory (product), and any promotions we have currently. Let's pick out the one you want/define the program/service you want, and I will be happy to get you all the exact pricing information so that you can make a good decision. By the way, so that I can do that, let me ask you a couple of questions:"

1. Ask questions about what they are buying.
2. Ask questions about what they currently have.

2. *"What Are the Interest Rates / Terms?"*

Use the 5-step process with the following word track:

"Sure, I will be happy to get you several different options. We use or can refer you to many different lending institutions, which enables us to show you several alternatives. By the way, what source did you finance through before, and who you were considering this time? I'm sure they are an excellent source; however, I believe we will have even better alternatives for you. After you have settled on the product/service I will go over all your options and obviously if none are agreeable you can use other sources."

This is used in a situation where you may provide indirect lending for your product or service. If you do, it is always better for you to arrange the funding rather than leave it to the customer to do; because if you leave it to outside influence too many negatives can occur that may cause you to lose the sale. You want to give those terms *after* the customer has selected their product or service, and not before whenever possible. When too much information is involved in the decision process too quickly, it clouds the overall process and creates numerous objections too soon. The order of the sales process can be very important logically and emotionally.

3. *"I Need Your Best Quote (RFP-Request for Proposal)."*

Use the 5-step process with the following word track:

"Absolutely, thanks for giving me the opportunity. I am positive that when you see what we have to offer, it will make a difference. So that I can give the best proposal, let me ask you a few questions."

1. Ask profiling questions.
2. Give your SDP (Specific Defining Proposition) based upon your customer.

3. Think apples to oranges. Change the game. Don't be a commodity. Do this by changing the decision-making criteria—change the terms, you, the packaging, the delivery, the servicing, the guarantee, the risk, and anything else you can think of. Every product or service can be commoditized or differentiated; it's up to you to figure out how.

4. *"I Want to Buy it for Cost/Invoice."*

Use the 5-step process with the following steps and word tracks:

"Sure, I understand. We all want the best price or value. Let's define the product/service you want, and work on that."

1. Change the decision criteria if possible. Again—think apples to oranges.
2. Think education versus selling. Educate your customers with valuable items and services, versus simply selling. Provide special reports titled "Ten things everyone should know before buying" or, "Ten things businesses don't want you to know when you buy/purchase."
3. Use the cost + profit example. "Mr. Customer, everything sold has a cost and a profit. First, you take the original cost and then you add expenses such as rent, interest, material costs, and so on—and then you have real cost. Next, you add a profit to define a selling price. The only real variable is: What is a fair profit? The State of Ohio charges 7.5 percent sales tax profit on everything you buy. They are not in the business, and they don't have the overhead of our business. If I were to use that profit margin on top of my true cost would that make sense to you?"

   Obviously, you have to create your own analogy for justifying your price that would make sense and work mathematically. Whatever analogy you use combines logic and emotion, and provides something mentally tangible that aids the customer in understanding price. Sometimes, when you negotiate, it is necessary for you to set the top and bottom parameters. In other words—you set the asking price and you set the bottom possible value in the customer's mind, and then negotiate between the two.

   Here is another situation where this might occur: A customer wants to buy a vehicle, but does not want to pay retail sticker price. As the salesperson, you can explain that the vehicles are now value-priced—which means that the vehicles have a lot less mark-up than ever before. This pricing strategy was created by the manufacturers to give customers fairer pricing and eliminate most of the negotiating. The good news is that the sticker price is often fairer; but the bad news is that most customers still expect to negotiate larger amounts than what is available. You now would offer a possible solution to the customer. "Mr. Customer, the base price before option is $20,000 and the optional equipment is an additional $3,000. The base price is a value price. Where you can have some flexibility is in the optional equipment. Can you and I propose a 10 percent discount on the $3,000 worth of optional equipment?"

What you are attempting to do in this example is first establish the value of your original price, whereby you are able to justify a lower negotiated value. You have also taken the price consideration from the $20,000 to the optional equipment of $3,000. It is easier to negotiate on $3,000 than $20,000, and it is easier to negotiate 10 percent of $3,000 than of $20,000. You have established the boundaries of your negotiations.

Some of you may be wondering how—since you sell a different service or product—the process of negotiating on a vehicle could possibly help you in working with your own product or service. Keep in mind that the same principles apply. Think of how to match these concepts to how you can, rather than mismatch them as to how you can't.

There is a lot less negotiating done for goods and services in the United States than in other countries. In many foreign nations, negotiating on just about everything—including the food that is bought—is simply a way of life. Because people in the United States don't grow up honing the habit of negotiating, they often view negotiating as an unappealing and troublesome activity. The reality is that everyone negotiates in some fashion everyday. **Just as "sales" is not a dirty word, neither is negotiating.**

4. Think value added. Beyond what the customers are buying from you, what can you do for their business? Can you provide alliances, leads, or solutions for other problems they have? Don't just think linear. Look at their total picture and help to solve their problems and eliminate their pain.

Five Lessons I Learned at Starbucks

Once after speaking at a conference in San Francisco, I found myself writing while sitting by a window in a busy Starbucks close to Union Square. It's funny what you can learn when you take the time to really observe and listen. I would like to share the five lessons I learned at Starbucks that can help you look at the bigger picture.

Lesson 1 – Make sure you ask for the business, and communicate with confidence. I watched as a beggar collected at least $5 worth of donations in a half hour, with a sign that said: "I am saving up for a hooker, weed, wine, and a steak dinner." Not one of the people who gave this man money bothered to read his sign. None of them knew what they were donating money towards—not the family man with his wife and children, not the group of older people who were likely in their 80s, not the business man in the suit—nobody. The beggar obviously learned the power of asking, no matter what. He had total confidence as he asked while he smiled.

Lesson 2 – It's not the money. People pile into Starbucks one after another and spend three to five bucks on of a cup coffee. Obviously, you can get a cup of coffee at a diner down the street for a lot less money. Yet people willingly spend $100 per month or more at Starbucks. Why?

Because people are buying the experience and the perception of the brand. I sat there, people-watching in a busy Starbucks, when I could have been in the quiet and seclusion of my nice hotel room. The person in the seat next to me was listening to music on an iPod, when they could obviously do it for free in the Square with a less expensive cup of coffee. The gentleman in the big living room type chair was reading a novel. People want the experience. Understand the value that your customer wants, and the issue of money will become less important. The big three automakers gave huge rebates on their vehicles, and import vehicle manufacturers still kicked their butts—because customers paid more for more perceived value. It's not just about the money.

Lesson 3 – Change the process to win. I gazed out the window as people scurried on the streets. The whole world is moving faster today; the Internet, news, businesses, and people in general are moving at increasingly rapid speeds. People will willingly pay a lot of money for a process that either speeds things up or slows things down. Although many people want the former, just as many are fighting brain drain because of all the speed, and desire to have things slow down even more so. Change your process with your customers in mind, sell your unique advantage and experience to the customer—and they will pay for the process.

Lesson 4 – Change the wrapping. I stayed at a smaller but kind of funky and cool hotel in San Francisco. Because I travel so much and stay in so many look-a-like chain hotels, it's a treat to stay somewhere unique. In the last several years there has been a big push towards businesses upgrading and improving their facilities. Because I am in and out of so many businesses, it's nice when you see one that has tried to put a unique touch on what they do and how they look.

Have you ever visited a McDonalds in a city with strict rules that require the restaurant to change their usual outside appearance in order to be in tune with the local environment and culture? Chances are that it made you look twice and say, "Oh that's cool—a non-McDonalds McDonalds." Your product or service can elicit the same reaction by looking just a bit different than what your customers might be expecting.

Lesson 5 – The money is in the niche. Watching traffic go by in San Francisco makes you understand the wide array of cultures, diversity, and the multitude of options people desire in their choices. I am often puzzled as to why so many business people are led by advertising agencies to spend vast sums of money trying to be everything to everyone with a generic, non-benefit driven message. I often think that employees and managers would be better served to park their car across the street from their businesses, and just watch for an hour. Next, I think business owners would be well-served to drive the streets of where their customers live and look at what they buy, what they do, and who your customers really are. By physically putting yourself in your customer's place, you can truly find out what they want and need.

Who knew you could learn so much at Starbucks?

Now that we've delved into the actions that are more than worth taking, let's recap some common mistakes to avoid:

■ Showing sympathy versus empathy

When you show empathy, you understand the customers' problems and want to assist them in finding a solution. But when you simply show sympathy, you take on the customer's burdens and problems as your own. You own their problems, and because of this, you rarely will do the tough things necessary to help your customers help themselves. You will believe any and all excuses. I am going to tell you something that may shock you; it may want to make you even get out of the sales profession. But it's true; some customers will even lie to you! Shocking huh? Empathy is good. Sympathy will bury you.

■ Asking too many closed-ended questions

Seventy to eighty percent of your questions should be open-ended, not closed-ended. Open-ended questions do not lead to yes or no answers, but rather invoke conversation with the potential buyer.

■ Neglecting the spouse/decision maker

My wife is often ignored by salespeople when we go shopping together; and usually, she is the actual buyer. Always ask who the primary user is, and if there are any secondary users. If there are secondary users, ask if they will be involved in the selection process (Don't use the word "decision." You will be asking your customer to lie to you.). Here is a tip that involves appropriate gender selling methods. Women make over 50 percent of the purchases. Women influence 75 percent of all decisions, and if you are a man, women may control 100 percent of your happiness. Never ignore the power of a woman.

Quick Tip: Men who tell you they can make a buying decision without their wives often can't go to the bathroom without her approval. It usually helps to have the spouse involved. On the other hand, never offend a woman by suggesting that the involvement of her spouse or significant other is necessary for her to make a buying decision.

■ Disagreeing with your customer

Lose the battle, and win the war. Don't win an argument and lose a customer.

■ Selling products or services without selling yourself

People must buy *you* before they buy the product or service.

■ Displaying a lack of enthusiasm

If you are apathetic about your product or service, your customers will likely not care about it either. But if you get excited, they will too.

■ Asking financial data too soon and in the wrong way

Value precedes price. Use the question funnel—start with small questions first, and graduate to bigger issue questions.

■ Pre-qualifying

Don't make assumptions about who can or cannot buy. Billionaires wear jeans and t-shirts too.

■ Over-qualifying

Your job is to help the customer buy; not give reasons as to why they can't.

Objection Overruled!

Let's talk about the three types of customer objections, and the ways in which you can respond to each.

Three Categories of Objections
- Money
- Me
- Machine (product or service)

Types of Objections
- Emotional vs. Rational
- Spoken vs. Unspoken
- Real vs. Invalid

Emotional vs. rational objections. Customers react in one of three ways when they have an objection—like a parent, a child, or an adult.

Parent – This customer acts like your parent and scolds you while doing so. "Mr. Salesperson, I told you I would not go back and forth with your price proposal."

Child – This customer reacts by acting like an irrational child and may even lose their temper. They want to believe that all salespeople are crooks.

Adult – This customer reacts by acting like a rational adult, and may even tell you that while they appreciate your actions, they are not quite sold and need to keep shopping. Just realize that many customers in any environment, even corporate, can act emotionally. Don't follow their lead. Keep you cool and offer solutions to the problem, rather than talking about the problem itself.

Most customers who react emotionally and irrationally will begin to feel a sense of reciprocity to you if you don't react in the same way. The customer will often begin to feel a tinge of guilt for overreacting, and begin to be more conciliatory towards you and your offer.

Spoken versus unspoken objections. A high percentage of customers' objections are never communicated to you. You have to flush the objections out by asking questions about money, me, and the product/service. You need to then break down the objection to understand each element.

Real versus invalid objections. Customers can experience buying anxiety. The apprehension about their decision becomes so great that they choose to give camouflaged objections to mask the real objection. Dig deeper, dig deeper, dig deeper—and keep providing alternatives.

6-Step Method to Handle Objections
1. **Listen.** Notice that this is always first, and always essential.
2. **Agree.** You catch more flies with honey. Let the customer know that you see things his way.

3. **Test.** *"Is this something that would keep you from purchasing?"*
4. **Funnel.** *"Other than that, is there anything else that would keep you from purchasing?"* (Don't handle more than one objection at a time.)
5. **Address.** Have a word track or method for each common objection. (We will offer some examples later in the chapter.).
6. **Redirect.** Ask questions, and move on.

How A No Becomes a Yes

■ **"I want to think it over."** — If you were to observe a husband and wife who were looking to purchase a product or service—or a corporate team of purchasing directors—you would find that as soon as the salesperson leaves after the presentation and they are alone, they will begin to discuss their real fears and objections. Rarely, if ever, do people really think things over.

If a husband and wife look at a house they are considering buying and then tell the agent, "Let us talk about it, and we will get back with you," you can rest assured that they already know exactly what would make them want to buy or not buy the property. The couple does not go home and look at each other and say "Honey, let's take an hour and sit down and think about the house." The "I want to think it over" line is almost always an excuse or a delay. Superstar salespeople don't accept excuses without investigation. Weak salespeople allow the excuse and give it validity. Weak salespeople play mind games about how close they are to a sale, and begin to count commissions not yet earned from their "mind deals."

There is an old phrase, "Customers don't say no; they are really saying no not now, I don't have enough information." Often, the customer just lacks enough reassurance to know that they are not making a mistake. They need more information that would help to eliminate their fears. As a salesperson, you must begin with a process to investigate those fears and move forward.

Example
Step 1. "Absolutely Mr. Customer. How long will you need—a week, a month?"

Step 2. "I understand and I know how you feel; a lot of my customers have felt the same way when buying. Usually, once they have gotten enough information, they have found it easier to be comfortable going forward."

Step 3. "One thing I have found with most of my customers is that whether you take ten minutes or ten days to make a decision, it's more about how comfortable you feel with everything—and not how long you take. Wouldn't you agree?"

Step 4. "Mr. Customer, there are usually three things most people consider. One is what you are buying, two is who you are buying from, and three is the price or budget of what you are buying."

Step 5. "Is everything okay with me? Have I done anything to offend you; or is there anything else I can provide or do for you?"

Step 6. "Is there anything you would change about the product or service?"

Step 7. "Mr. Customer, if those things are okay then it's usually about the budgets and monies. I certainly can appreciate that. Money is obviously very important. Let me ask you a silly question: If this product or service were one dollar, would we be doing business right now? If so, then I think that tells us you are okay with the product/ service and me, and you need to be more comfortable with the money."

Step 8. "Let me ask one more silly question, if this were your dream or fantasy deal, what would the price, terms, or budgets be for you?"

Let's break down this format for handling the "I'll think it over customer." Usually, salespeople will ask the customer what they have to think over. The nature of this question forces the customer into a defensive mode, and he avoids the real answer. He moves more quickly to get away from you (the salesperson.) Your question compels the customer to feel threatened. Although I usually don't condone asking for the customer's position first as it relates to money, as a last resort of "I'll think it over objections," then I believe you should. The idea is to get the customer through non-threatening logic and emotion to state their position before they leave you. In this case, it is better to flush out any objections and even get the customer to state lower than possible prices, terms, and conditions, than to have the customer not state the objections at all. When customers make a commitment to buy right then—no matter the terms—they become much more flexible in those terms. Their ability to see themselves as buyers or owners produces emotions that lead to flexibility. In other words, *"Emotions distort reality."*

- "Your price is too high!"

Use the step method for objections and the following ideas:

"I appreciate what you are saying. Let me ask you, when you say too high, do you mean too high for the product itself, too high versus others, or too high for your budget?"

Always break down objections. What you think might be an objection might really be a complaint or a stall; or it may be a protest to budget or terms.

"I appreciate that Mr. Customer; I am never the cheapest. Cheap things aren't good, and good things aren't cheap. However, I invite you to consider the notion that price is what you pay, value is what you receive, and your true cost is the difference between the two. Simply being the cheapest price usually never equals having the lowest cost; and the cheapest price almost always has the cheapest value. The old adage of 'you get what you pay for' is true. Have you—like me—ever bought something because it was the cheapest price; and lived to really regret that decision? I'm sure that we all have. It's better to pay a little more now and get what you deserve than to pay a little less and get something cheap that you don't deserve."

"I understand, Mr. Customer. Let me ask you a question: What if the product/service were free and there were no price considerations—would you purchase it from me? Obviously, nothing is free; but if you receive a tremendous amount of value from us that you don't get elsewhere, it's a much better investment, isn't it? "It's better to pay a little more than you expected now than to pay a little less than you should, and regret it later."

Other Closes:

1. *Assumptive Close*

"When did you want us to install the product?"

"How did you want to register and title the vehicle?"

2. *Alternative Choice Assumptive Close*

"Will that be check or credit card?"

"Are you taking this with you, or will we be delivering it?"

"Will you issue the purchase order, or do I need to get that from the accounting department?"

"Will we be starting this campaign this quarter or next?"

3. *Question with a Question Close*

"Do you have it in blue?" "Let me check for you. Is blue the only color you were looking for, or are you looking at other colors as well?"

4. *Pictured Involvement Close*

"Just picture pulling up to the golf course in your new vehicle and pulling out your clubs; imagine how easy it will be to get them out of this trunk."

"Picture how your boss will feel when you increase productivity and the bottom line with this product/service."

"Picture the look on your family's faces when they are sitting on the couch watching a movie in high definition and listening to the surround sound."

5. Order Close

"Just put your okay right here by the checkmark."

6. Clarify Close

"Obviously, you have a good reason for saying that or feeling that way. May I ask what that may be?"

7. Difference in Budget Close

The $500 a month payment vs. the $400 a month current payments should be presented as +$100. Your customer has already bought into the $400 a month budget; so don't resell the whole budget, only the increase.

8. Residual Value Close

"Mr. Customer, if you have a 40 percent residual value in three years with this product, then you are really only paying for the difference between the beginning value and that residual if you wish to trade this in. The good news is this product has a very high residual value because of its strong overall value. Look at overall ownership cost."

9. Puppy Dog Close

If you take a puppy home from the pet store, you don't want to take it back. Let your customers try you and your product or service on for size. Always offer a slice or sample of your product or offer a risk-free or money-back guarantee. I personally have a program that I offer that is not only money back but that I will pay the customer $10,000 for their troubles if they don't want to keep the program after 90 days.

When people commit to and start to enjoy the puppy, they don't want to take it back.

10. Lost Sale Close

"Have I done anything to offend you? Is there anything else I can do, or do differently than what I have done?"

11. Minor/Major Close

"Are you financing or paying cash?" (The answering of this minor question automatically answers the major question that they are buying.)

12. Logic Close

"Mr. Customer, would you agree that you would be saving money on the increased fuel mileage with this vehicle? You are also getting a vehicle that has a full warranty versus your current one, which does not have any warranty left. You are going to face higher maintenance and repair costs with an older vehicle—would you agree? When you consider these savings and overall costs, you would actually pay more to stay in an old vehicle than to get into a brand new one."

13. Guaranteed Depreciation Close for Leasing

"Mr. Customer, the moment you take delivery of your new copier, how much will it depreciate? The next year—how much? The third year—how much? How much are you willing to pay to own something with little resale value? Let's look at a lease alternative, and then you can decide which is best for you."

14. *I Got Your Price Beat Close*

"I understand Mr. Customer; if money were the same, who would you rather do business with?" (They usually will say you, unless they hate you for some reason at this point.) Now ask them why. When they reply, then ask them why else. Keep asking them why else until they are out of answers. Write every reason down, and then show these reasons to the customer. Remind them that each reason has a value, and that they have just shown themselves exactly why they should do business with you."

15. *Power of Three Close*

As discussed previously, when you are showing money, budgets, or terms—always give three options. People love choice and three is the perfect number for choice. One is take it or leave it; and two is either/or, but leaves doubt. Three is just perfect; more choices than this are too many.

16. *Ben Franklin Close*

"Ben Franklin had a simple system for making decisions. He simply wrote the pluses and minuses on a paper, and weighed them out." Draw a t-bar on a piece of paper, and put a plus on the left-hand side and a minus on the right-hand side. Begin to write down all the positive points for the customer. After you've cited several, look up at the customer and tell them you think they have already made their decision.

17. *Spouse Stall Close*

"Mr. Customer, do you think your spouse would potentially object to the product/service or the money?" (This helps to narrow the potential objection.) If the objection is money—which it usually is—ask if by money, they mean the budgets, such as payments and down payments. Ask the customer: "If I can make the money the same or better than your current budget, would your spouse object then?" Show how the product or service provides warranty, productivity increases, less maintenance, and more. As a last resort, you can close the subject until the spouse's approval.

18. *Second-Party Assist Close*

If the buyer has a second party assisting and counseling them at the time of proposal and close, ask the second party what they would suggest the buyer do—knowing that their opinion is important. You are taking the calculated risk that because you valued the second party's opinion, he will in turn reciprocate and assist you; rather than fight you.

19. *Delay Payment Close*

Most people are optimistic that their world will be better tomorrow than today. When you offer a delayed first payment or financial obligation, the customer lets their optimism enter into the decision process. Breathing room allows a decision to be made more easily. People feel pressure today, but often not in the future.

20. *Buy Down Close*

If you provide indirect lending and can buy down the interest rate, you can entice certain customers to justify their decision. People have become more and more interest-rate conscious in their buying activities.

21. *Cash Back Close*

Cash is king. If you can offer cash rebates, you have a better chance of closing successfully, since customers tend to love cash in their hands.

You can also offer cash payments for equity that has accrued in tradable items.

22. *House in Los Angeles Lease Close*

a. Draw a house.
b. "Imagine buying a house in Los Angeles a few years back; let's say it was $300,000."
c. "Do you remember the years that there were fires, floods, mudslides, earthquakes, riots, the OJ Simpson case, the Reginald Denny beating, and the Menendez brother's murders in Los Angeles?"
d. "The average house dropped quickly in value."
e. "If you were the buyer, and could have seen that those things were going to happen, what would you have done?"
   1. Buy the house and pay cash if you had it?
   2. Buy the house and finance it?
   3. Lease the house and only pay for what you used?

"Mr. Customer, the buying examples cause you to lose a lot of equity quickly; the leasing example does not."

23. *Re-Demonstration Close*

This is one of the easiest, least-frequently used, and probably most effective closes. When your sales process is stalled, always re-demonstrate the product or service to reacquaint the customer with its value, and the emotions that it stirred in the customer.

24. *Other than Close*

Set aside issues by saying, "Other than that, is there anything else that would keep you from purchasing?" This allows you to isolate any objection.

25. *Exact Number Close*

$176,947 lends more validity than $175,000. Don't round numbers; give customers exact figures.

26. *Reduce to the Ridiculous Close*

$50 a month is $1.66 a day, or a couple of Cokes a day. Explain it in the smallest terms possible.

27. *Referral Close*

"I would consider your proposal if you can provide me with the names and numbers of two prospective customers who are likely to be in the market for this product or service."

28. *Three Questions Close*

a. Do you like it?
b. Do you see the value in it?
c. Do you want it?

29. *Money Equal Close*

"If the price were the same, who would you rather do business with?" (Have the customer build your case.)

30. *Fear of Loss Close*

"If you don't buy today, and someone else buys the house, then it just wasn't meant to be."

31. Test Close

"That would not keep you from buying today—would it?"

32. Admit Close

Use in response to a "price is too high" objection. "It is high, isn't it?" Be quiet, and find the strength of conviction. Find out if the customer is testing you or they truly believe the price is too high.

33. You Can Afford It Close

"You can afford it, and you deserve it."

34. Silent Close

Make an offer, ask for the business, and shut up.

35. Leave Alone Close

"Let me leave you two alone so you can decide."

36. Future Close

    a. "If you buy today, where do you go from here?"
    b. "Where do you see yourself 90 days from now?"
    c. "If you were to buy in the future, what would have to happen?"

37. Risk Reversal Close

    a. "If you had a guarantee, what would that guarantee look like; and would it make a difference?"

b. "If you could propose one thing to lower your risk to be able to do business, what would that one thing be?"

38. *Not Today Close*

a. "When you decide to wait, that's as much a decision as deciding to buy today."
b. "The hardest part of getting what you want is deciding to do so."

39. *Judgment Close*

"Mr. Customer, I would like to make a deal with you, and ask that you don't judge me by your last bad salesperson—and I won't judge you by my last bad customer." (Say this with a smile on your face, and inject some humor.)

40. *Perfect Time Close*

"There is never a perfect time; but this is the right time."

More Negotiating Techniques

a. **Flinch** – Flinch when you receive an offer to plant a seed of doubt in the customers mind.

- "Wow!"
- "Really?"
- "I didn't expect that."

b. **Bracket proposals** – Counter-offer the customer proposals by offering the same amount above your desired position as they offered below your desired position.

c. **Vice** – "It will take more than that, Mr. Customer." A customer may test you with a counter-offer to your proposal. When a customer makes a counter offer, you can forcefully plant a seed of doubt to his offer by telling him that the offer is too low, too high, that it will take more than that, or that you appreciate his offer—but it's not close enough to consider. You are squeezing a vice-grip on their counter offer.

d. **Salami technique** – Negotiate a part, rather than a whole. Cut the decision into small pieces.

e. **Take away** – After a customer offers you a low price, offer to take away several components of the purchase for that price. People want what they can't have, and they will negotiate for it. This technique takes the focus away from just price.

f. **Split the difference of price or terms** – Always state this as the customer's idea: "Mr. Customer, why don't you propose to split the difference of our prices?"

g. **Declining concessions** – When giving more than one concession in the course of negotiating, always make sure that each concession is of less value than the previous concession. This shows an ending direction to the negotiations.

h. **Counter first offer—**
   ■ Never accept the first offer from a customer.
   ■ Never accept an offer too eagerly.
   Both can create doubt in the customer's mind as to how good their offer really was.

I. **Varied concessions** – If you must concede more than once during negotiations, vary the amounts of the concessions.

J. **Give-Get** – Always get something in return when you give something up. This stops the customer from asking and maintains profits.

k. **Add Value** – If a customer asks for money discounts, you can add some form of value instead of a discount – such as equipment, goods, guarantees, or services.

I have seen many salesmen who could make impressive first impressions, create good rapport with customers, and do great presentation/demonstrations; but could not close a door. In many ways, fear kept those salespeople from becoming sales superstars. To be a sales superstar, you must perform at a high level on in all areas. Otherwise, you are like a football player who runs the ball 99 yards—and then stops on the one yard line. Negotiating and closing can often be that last yard of the sales process.

To be a sales superstar you must master sales, people, life, and marketing skills. The tough news is that it takes a lot of work. The good news is that very few salespeople will ever pay that price. Because of this, you can stand heads above your competition in sales and create success and riches most people only dream of. By using the contrarian information in this book, you can break all the rules of selling and become a sales superstar while doing it. I wish you the best in your venture—here is to you, and happy and successful sales superstardom!

To contact Mark Tewart for speaking engagements or to find out how he can assist you and your company in becoming sales superstars:

Call 888-2Tewart (888-283–9278) or 513-932–9526 or email info@ tewart.com.

www.marktewart.com
www.marktewart.com/blog
www.tewart.com
www.myspace.com/marktewart

About the Author

Mark Tewart is an author, professional speaker, consultant, entrepreneur, and owner of several businesses. Mark is the author of 12 books including *How to Be a Sales Superstar: Break All the Rules and Succeed While Doing It* (John Wiley & Sons). Mark has published thousands of articles and has been interviewed in numerous magazines such as *Entrepreneur, RealtySuccess, Dealer Marketing,* and *AutoSuccess* to name a few. Mark is a professional member of the National Speakers Association and Authors Guild. Mark speaks to audiences worldwide on the topics of sales, sales marketing, sales management, and creating a high performance life.

Mark Tewart
Tewart Enterprises Inc—Tewart Management Group Inc.—Ninth & Main, LLC
307 East Silver St
Lebanon, Ohio 45036
888 2Tewart (888-283–9278)

To sign up for Mark's FREE newsletter and receive your FREE CD "6 Elements of Success,"(go to www.marktewart.com.)

Index

21 Times Approach, 112–113
3Ms, 168

A

Abraham, Jay, 129
Accountability, education and, 45
Action Management, Four Ds of, 80
Add Value, 224
Admit Close, 222
Advancement, sales and, 2–3
Advertising, outdated, 47
Adwords, 114
Affiliations, 101
Allison, Luther, 184
Alternative Choice Assumptive Close, 215
Appearance, 150
The Apprentice, 189–190
Assumptive Close, 215

Attitude:
 assessing your, 95–96
 gaining the right, 83–88
 maintaining the right, 88–92
 negative influences on, 92–95
Attraction, Law of, 63–65
Auditory learners, 40–41
automaticresponse.com, 126
Aviator, 31
aweber.com, 126

B

Baber, Anne, 172
Barnum, P.T., 117, 187–188
Believability, 178
Ben Franklin Close, 218
Bencivenga, Gary, 129
Benson, Richard, 129
Bird dog programs, 101
blifax.com, 126

Blogging, 101
  education and, 50–51
  follow ups and, 123
Bly, Robert, 129
Bottom line, five ways to
      increase the, 102–104
Bracket proposals, 223
Budget Close, Difference in, 216
Buffett, Warren, 7
Burgin, David, 23
Business cards, unique, 115–116
Buy Down Close, 219
Buzz marketing, 116
Bypass technique:
  avoiding the, 154
  proposal stage and, 200–201

C

Calls, 78–79
  personal, follow ups and, 123
  targeted phone, 101
Caples, John, 129
Carnegie Mellon, 5
Carson, Johnny, 171
Cash Back Close, 219
Cell phones, 78–79
Children:
  inspiration and, 34
  sales skills, 3
Chinian, Paul, 46
Chrysler, 122

cityblueprint.com, 126
Clarify Close, 216
Clinton, Bill, 173–174
Coca Cola, 7
Communication plan, for current
      customers, 124–125
Community boards, 101
Competence:
  confidence and, 39, 137
  proposal stage, 203
  unconscious, 138
Concessions, declining and
      varied, 224
Confidence, competence and,
      39, 137
  proposal stage, 203
Contrarian Method:
  competence and, 137
  vs. contrary, 7–11
  mystery shopping and, 48–50
  proposal stage and, 200–201
  selection stage and, 189
Control, avoiding attempts to
      gain customer, 140
Countering first offers, 224
Coupon swaps, 101
Criticism, attitude toward, 92
Customers:
  be-back, 101, 110–111
  conquest, 120
  disagreeing with, 210
  lost, 101

orphan, 101
prioritizing current,
    119–122
  add-ons and continuity,
    130–132
  effective communication
    with, 122–128
  getting them to sell for you,
    132–134
  mistakes made with follow
    ups, 128–129
  yearly market evaluations
    for, 129–130
repeat buyers, 101

D

Dairy Queen, 7
Database marketing, 101
Deadline, goals without, 31
Dealer Twenty Groups, 47
Decision maker, neglecting
    the, 209
Delay Payment Close, 219
Delegation, 75
Depreciation Close for Leasing,
    Guaranteed, 217
Desire, goal-setting and, 56
Digg. *See* Social networks
Douglas, Michael, 134
Downloads, education and, 45
draw-me.com, 126

E

eBay, 113–114
Education, 35–36
  changing customer base
    and, 9
  continuing, 13
  customized, 106
  experts, seeking out, 50–51
  group, 43–48
  learning modalities, 40–43
  measurements and, 51–54
  motivation and, 37–38
  mystery shopping, 48–50
  vs. training, 38–39
Email, 101
  autoresponder, 123
  newsletters and education,
    50–51
  video, 123
Emerson, Ralph Waldo, 63
Emotions:
  objections based on, 211
  profiling and, 164–169
  roadblocks and negative, 23
Environment. *See* Selection
    stage, setting the
    environment
Exact Number Close, 220
Exercise, as an attitude booster,
    87–88
ezinequeen.com, 126

F

FaceBook. *See* Social networks
Familiarity, Law of, 21,
         161, 166
Faxes, follow ups and, 123
Fear: *See also* Loss Close,
         Fear of
  profiling and, 167–168
  roadblocks and, 21–23
FedEx, 142, 198
Fifty Calls, 71
Filtering, goal, 59
firststream.com, 126
Flinch, 223
Fluctuations, marketing and,
         98–99
Flyers, 101
Focus group, 188
Ford, 122
Four Ds of Action Management.
         See Action Management,
         Four Ds of
Franklin, Benjamin. *See* Ben
         Franklin Close
Frequent buyer programs, 123
Future Close, 222

G

Garfinkel, David, 129
General Motors, 122
Gestalt psychology, 21

Gifts:
  follow ups and, 123
  unique, 144
Give-Get, 224
GlenGarry Glen Ross, 139
Goal-setting:
  belief and, 65–67
  clear vision, 57–62
  ineffective, 55–57
  power of now and, 62–65
Godin, Seth, 116
Google, 114
grandincentives.com, 126
Gratification, rule of instant, 119
Great Connections, 172
Greed, money and, 25–26
Green Bay Packers, 36
Greetings, 146
  to profiling, 155–158
Gretzky, Wayne, 50

H

Habits, daily, 61–62
Halbert, Gary, 129
Handshake, 146–147
handymailing.com, 126
Hansen, Mark Victor, 51, 64
Happiness, money and, 24–25
HFG (Hope for Gain), 45, 167
High Point University, 38
Hill, Napoleon, 89
Honesty, 178

HOPE (Having Optimistic
Predictions and
Emotions), 14
goal-setting and, 63
Hopkins, Claude, 104, 129, 184
*How to Write a Great
Advertisement,* 129
Hughes, Howard, 31
Hurricane Katrina, 84

I

IBM, 37
Immigrants, wealth and, 27
Index card system, 78
infusion.com, 126
Instant messaging, follow ups
and, 123
Interest rates/terms, questions
concerning, 204
internetaudioguy.com, 126
internetvideoguy.com, 126
Invalid objections, 211
Investment, mental, 6
Isolation, 46

J

The Jeffersons, 167
JOB (Just Over Broke), 70
Job mission, 154–155
Joint venture advertising, 101
Jordan, Michael, 14

Judgment Close, 223
Justification, logic and, 179–180

K

Kennedy, Dan, 51, 99, 129
Kinesthetic learners, 40–41
Kiyosaki, Robert, 5

L

Land Rover, 190–191
Language:
buyers, 104
getting attention through, 73
Lead generation. *See* Marketing
skills
Leads, sources of, 100–101
Leave Alone Close, 222
Lemmings, unsuccessful
salespeople as, 8
Letters, follow ups and, 123
Leverage, marketing, 104–105
Lexus, 180, 190
Life skills, 12–13
action management and, 70
Listening skills, 12
Logic Close, 217
Lombardi, Vince, 19, 36, 193
Los Angeles Lease Close, House
in, 220
Los Angeles Times, 62
Loss Close, Fear of, 221

Lost Keys Close, 168
Lost Sale Close, 217
Lumpy mail. *See* Mail,
    multidimensional
lumpymail.com, 126
Lynch, Damon, 183–184

M

Mailings:
    follow ups and, 123
    multidimensional, 114–115
    targeted list, 101
Maltz, Maxwell, 53
Management:
    attitude and, 93
    views of contrarians, 8
Marketing skills, 13–14,
        97–100
    Be-Back CD, 110–111
    business cards, 115–116
    buzz marketing, 116–117
    creating a marketing web,
        100–107
    desirable areas, 112–113
    direct mail, 114–115
    eBay, 113–114
    pay-per-click methods, 113
    persistence, 109–110
    Reverse Funnel Theory,
        107–109
    special announcements, 113

and your neighbors, friends,
        and relatives, 111–112
MBA degrees. *See* Education
McDonalds, 208
mcmannisduplication.com, 126
Measurements:
    education and, 51–54
    time management and, 72–76
Meet and greets, 146–151
Mentoring, 45
    education and, 47–48
Michaels, Al, 32
Mind's eye, goal-setting and, 57
Minor/Major Close, 217
Money:
    beginning salespeople and
        focus on, 70
    importance of happiness and,
        24–25
    misconceptions about, 25–26
    savings and, 27–28
    television and movie
        portrayals of, 26–27
    value and, 25
Money Equal Close, 221
moreson.com, 126
Motivation, 37–38
Multitasking, negative results
        of, 77
*My Life in Advertising and Scientific
        Advertising,* 129, 184

myspace.com, 37–38, 126. *See also* Social networks
Mystery shopping, 39, 48–50

N

Names, exchanging, 147
National Automobile Dealers Association, 120, 138–139
National Speakers Association, 193
Needs, goal-setting and, 56
News, negative influences of, 85–87
Newsletters, follow ups and, 123
The New York Times, 62
Nicholas, Ted, 129
Nike, 191
nohasslenewsletters.com, 126
Not Today Close, 223

O

Obligation, theory of, 148
Observation skills, 12
Obstacles. *See* Roadblocks
Optimism, goal-setting and, 62
Order Close, 216
orientaltrading.com, 126
Other than Close, 220
Outsourcing, 75
Over-The-Rhine Riots, 183
Ownership, pride of, 180–181

P

Pac Man, 87–88
Pain, goal-setting and, 56
Parkinson's Law, 94
Patterns:
  goal-setting, 58
  repeaters, 21
  of success, 76–77
Pay-per-click method, 114
PDAs, 78
People skills, 12
Perception, 157
  selection stage and, 185
Perfect Time Close, 223
Performance, 180
Philosophy, importance of personal, 18
Pictured Involvement Close, 215
Postcards, follow ups and, 123
Present, importance of, 62–65
Presentations, 144. *See also* Selection stage
Price, questions concerning best, 203–204
Pride, 6
Proactive, vs. reactive, 11
Profiling, 155–158
  vs. qualifying, 158–162
  sample questions, 162
Promotion announcements, job, 113

Proof, social, 176
Proposal stage, 197–198
  alternative closes, 215–223
  customer questions/
      comments, 199–203
    typical questions, 203–208
    common mistakes,
      208–210
  objections, 210–214
  other negotiating techniques,
    223–225
Protection, 181
Proxemics, 147–148
Psycho-Cybernetics, 53
psychologicaltriggers.com, 129
Psychology:
  Gestalt, 21
  profiling and, 164–169
Puppy Dog Close, 216–217
Purple Cow, 116

Q

Qualifying:
  over-, 210
  pre-, 210
  vs. profile, 158–162
Quebin, Nido, 38, 51
Question Close, 215
Questioning:
  4Ps, 180–182
  as conversation, 171–173

deal-killers, 162–164
open-ended vs. closed-ended,
    172–173
positive words/phrases, 173–174
for profiling, 162
underlying meaning of,
    175–180
See also Proposal stage,
    customer questions/
    concerns
Quote, questions concerning
    best, 204–205

R

Rational objections, 211
Reading, importance of, 41–43
Real objections, 211
Reciprocity, Law of, 107, 148
Re-Demonstration Close, 220
Reduce to the Ridiculous
    Close, 221
Referral Close, 221
Referrals, 101
  follow ups and, 123
Rejection, attitudes about,
    90–92
Reluctance, 1–2
Residual Value Close, 216
Reverse Funnel Theory,
    107–109
RFPs (Requests for Proposal), 197

Rich Dad Poor Dad, 5

Risk, aversion and reversal, 105
  profiling and, 168

Risk Reversal Close, 222–223

Roadblocks:
  breaking through, 28–29
  destroying, 23–26
  identifying, 19–23

Robert, Cavett, 193

Rohn, Jim, 51

Rohn, John, 37

RPMs (Recent Positive
      Moments), 32–33
  goal-setting and, 59–60

RSS feeders, 50–51, 123

Ruby, Jeff, 156–157

S

Salami technique, 224

Sales Esteem, 181

Sales process, pros and cons,
      135–140

Sales skills. *See specific skills*

Scarcity, 106

Schwab, Victor, 129

SDP (Specific Defining
      Proposition), 175

Second-Party Assist Close, 219

*Secrets of Successful Direct
      Mail,* 129

Selection stage, 183–186

assumptive stage and, 194–196
five keys to peak performance,
      192–194
presentations, 187–192
setting the environment,
      186–187

Seminars, 45
  to get appointments, 141–142

sendoutcards.com, 75, 126

Service departments, 101

Setbacks. *See* Roadblocks

Shopping. *See* Mystery shopping

Silent Close, 222

Social networks, 101

Software, appointment, 78

Speak and Grow Rich, 51

Spoken objections, 211

Spouse, neglecting the, 209

Spouse Stall Close, 218–219

Spray and Pay Method, 165

SRDS (Standard Rate and Data
      Service), 112

Starbucks, 207–208

Stereotypes, 3–4

Stories:
  future based, 177
  similar situation, 176–177
  testimonials, 177

Subconscious, goals and, 30

Success:
  skills of, 69–70
  three currencies of, 69

Sugarman, Joe, 129
Suzuki, Shunryu, 33
Sympathy, vs. empathy, 209

T

Tags, 173–174
Take away, 224
Talent, 2, 14
    vs. attitude, 83–84
Tall Poppy Syndrome, 9
Teams, education and,
    43–48
Technology: *See also specific type*
    education and, 37–38
    experts and, 50–51
    time management and,
    77–79
Teleseminars, 45
Test Close, 221
Testimonials. *See* Stories,
    testimonials
Tewart Management Group
    Inc., 23
Text messages, 123
Think and Grow Rich, 89
Thoreau, Henry David, 67
Three Close, Power of, 218
Three Questions Close, 221
Tickets, service, 101
Time management:
    vs. action, 69–71

avoiding time wasters, 79–81
exposing lies of, 77–79
    accounting for habits and,
        71–72
    automating actions, 75
    ending undesirable actions,
        76–77
    expanding actions, 74
        through others, 74–75
    measuring
        bad results, 75
        good results, 72
    monitoring, 77
    recognizing actions that
        lead to good results,
        72–74, 76–77
Tin Men, 139
TLC (Think Like a Customer),
    39, 140, 143
Tone, 149
Toyota, 122, 180, 187
Training, vs. education, 38–39
Trump, Donald, 31, 189–190
Turnover, 45

U

UCLA Bruins, 36
Underachievement, reasons for,
    97–100
Uniqueness, 178
Universal Truths Statements/
    Questions, 147, 156

Unspoken objections, 211
USP (Unique Selling Proposition), 175

V

Vacations, importance of, 93–94
Value:
   money and, 25
   vs. price proposition, 106–107
Vice, 223–224
VIP memberships, follow ups and, 123
Visits, follow ups and personal, 123
Visual learners, 40–41
Voice messaging, follow ups and, 123

W

wallet-mailer.com, 126
Wall Street, 134

Walters, Dottie, 50–51
Walton, Bill, 36
Wayne, John, 182
Webinars, 45
Wedding announcements, 113
West, Bill, 92
When-Then Syndrome, 33, 99
Wooden, John, 36
Word track, 202
Word Tracker, 114
wordpress.com, 126
Writing, to improve speaking skills, 145–146

Y

You Can Afford It Close, 222

Z

Ziglar, Zig, 24, 37, 149, 175